COMPANY MAN
My Jesuit Life, 1950–1968

by Jim Bowman

A Blithe Spirit Publication
Oak Park, Illinois, 2012

in partnership with
Little Man Press. Chicago, IL

www.myjesuitlife.com
www.littlemanpress.wordpress.com

PRELIMINARY REMARKS:

Time flies. It seems like yesterday. The way it was. I remember when. So it goes.

The book at hand was intended at first for our children, a sort of family history as told by the father, and it retains the flavor of that. But it moved inevitably into the general-population arena, such is my habit from years of writing for the general population.

It includes a good deal of self-explanation, always a tricky matter. A straight description of the matter might have done nicely, a going easier on the first personal pronoun. But it is my story and not primarily anyone else's.

At the same time, it is also a story of Jesuit life, at least of the '50s and '60s, and of the church of those years.

Unless otherwise clear, the names are of Jesuits, in the naming of whom I have mostly dispensed with titles—"Rev.," "Fr." and the like. The informality stems from familiarity, not contempt, believe me.

As for the book's title, "Company of Jesus" was an early name for the Jesuits, now formally the Society of Jesus. The name has military overtones, to reflect the founder's military background, and suggests also being companions of Jesus. I was a company man in that respect as well as some others that may come to mind.

With the mother and the father; Oak Park, 1955.

ENDURING APPRECIATION OF:

The mother and the father, who nourished me, perhaps unwittingly, in the spiritual life, and the three brothers and a sister, who were part of that process.

The loving wife of 43 years and the six perfect children, for obvious reasons, not least in being a very special audience for this book, in that sense its inspiration.

The loving wife again, for reading the manuscript, questioning meaning and intent, and finding mistakes. She's a smart and sensitive lady, believe me.

The Jesuits I knew and some I didn't know: collectively they had a lot to do with what I am today, not that I'm blaming anyone. Two of them read the manuscript and encouraged me. They know who they are. Readers needn't.

Last but not least, my son the bookmaker, Peter D. Bowman, who designed the book.

CONTENTS:

CHAPTER 1. BOOT CAMP: NOVITIATE, 1950–1952

More things are wrought by prayer than this world dreams of.
—Alfred, Lord Tennyson

Five of us took the New York Central from Chicago to Cincinnati in August, 1950, arriving with hours to spare before our 6 p.m. novitiate-arrival deadline. Our destination was suburban Milford, 15 miles east of the city. Killing time, we cabbed it at one point. One of us wanted to buy a fielder's glove. We asked the cabbie where we could find a sporting goods place. He picked up on the sporting part and was about to suggest a brothel. We cut him short smilingly. Athletic goods, yes. Sexual athletics, no.

Milford was a village of a few thousand souls, on the Little Miami River. Across the river was the novitiate, a three-story brick institutional structure on 99 acres. Showing up with minutes to spare, smelling slightly of beer, we entered a sort of frat house existence, minus amenities, including beer. No more of that for four years.

We each arrived after a year of college, all but one of us destined to remain through priestly ordination, all but one of those to leave the order and the ministry. We brought the total of new men to 22 or so. Another 25 came a few weeks later, making a first-year novice class of close to 50—from Chicago, Cincinnati, Detroit, Cleveland, and elsewhere in five states including Indiana and Kentucky.

Those were palmy days for Jesuits, as for seminaries all over, what with 90-man novitiates and two-hundred-man "houses," counting Latin and Greek classics students on the other side of the big brick building, in their third and fourth years at Milford, plus brothers, faculty, and retirees. Catholics were not second-guessing themselves as they would 15 years later, especially seminarians, priests, and nuns. Among Milford novices, for instance, objections were personal, not institutional.

We missed "beer and babes," as one novice said—a sprightly fellow from downstate Illinois who would have been a barrel of fun in a bar. Some missed the lost ability to become fathers, which hadn't occurred to me and wouldn't, until I became one. Others, including me, missed the freedom to hang on the corner and watch the girls go by.

Not all of us missed girls, it turned out. The point did not arise, except in advice against forming "particular friendship," which in any case was presented more as an offense against community spirit than sexual carrying on.

THE FIRST DAYS

We became nine-to-fivers, to bed at nine and up at five, sleeping on cots in six-man dormitories, each in a curtained cubicle. Entering in early August, we met ferocious Ohio Valley heat and humidity. Curtains were drawn, six ceiling-high windows were thrown open. Next to each window was a desk where we would kneel for the daily hour of meditation, 5:30 to 6:30.

Not in the first few days. We had to learn how to meditate, which was more than saying a Hail Mary. One of us had been told that the two years of novitiate would be hell if we didn't learn how to pray, that is, as religious prayed, as Jesuits prayed. The novitiate was to be our introduction to a life of reflection. Ours was to be an examined life.

A second-year novice from downstate Illinois, our "spiritual father," gave us a motto of sorts: You succeed at prayer by trying. It's a prescription for mediocrity but recognized the difficulty and gave us a sort of pep-talk incentive. What did we know? He'd been doing prayer for a year.

BOYHOOD PREP

The prayer was meditation and not the petition I had made routinely during the war at bedtime, praying for peace and my brothers overseas or in preparation for an intramural boxing match. For a fight I used a saying of St. Ignatius which I had picked up somewhere and have since found it's as Jewish as it is Christian, not to mention Catholic: Pray as if everything depends on God, act as if everything depends on you. So I trained and got to bed early and in nightly prayer put my fate in God's hands. It was not a bad exercise. Indeed, I entered the Jesuits with precisely that purpose.

I ran into a local bully boy at Austin and Madison and told him I was joining the Jesuits. "Why on earth would you want to do that?" he asked, stunned. No less incredulous was friend George, who wondered the same thing. I told him I wanted to do something that gave me full guarantee of doing God's will. He heard me out respectfully. Friend Brad across the alley, who at one point considered joining the Trappists, resonated with my intention. We both had the habit of daily mass and communion at our parish church a few blocks from our houses.

Such a tidal wave of piety is worth noting. It came from inside the families, but also from school. In senior year at Fenwick High, in Oak Park, a Dominican school, we had a religion teacher who pushed the envelope for us with a taking-Scripture-seriously approach. Even friend Bill, skeptical toward the church in ways I was not, found this teacher, Father James Regan, OP, worth the entire $150 annual tuition, so engaging were his classes, which he taught half from Scripture and tradition, half from Time Magazine and other news outlets.

For instance, discussing Jesus' saying that the children of this world are wiser in their generation than the children of light, Father Regan brought up Franklin D. Roosevelt campaigning hatless in the rain in an open car, trying harder to gain his earthly crown than we to gain our heavenly, to use the language of that day's piety. Such an argument struck home for the adolescent listener with half an interest in discovering the meaning of life. It was the sort of thing that got Brad and me off to church on weekdays.

More specifically, Father Regan asked repeatedly in daily quizzes until it had sunk in to his satisfaction, What's priceless within easy reach every day? Holy Communion, of course. For the believing 17-year-old, it made perfect sense, especially for me who as a grade-schooler had gone to daily mass with my parents during the war, praying for the return of my brothers. It was a matter of home-fires burning with relentless piety, including nightly family rosary. Combine such home and family experience with formal instruction in a school atmosphere that drove home Catholic viewpoints and exuded faith and prayer, and you had a formula for encouraging the religious bent.

SISTER ALFRED RECOMMENDS

It started in grade school. Sister Mary Alfred, RSM (Sister of Mercy), recommended saying "aspirations" while waiting in line in church during confirmation practice. We knew what these were: short prayers such as "Jesus, meek and humble of heart, make my heart like unto mine" or "Sacred Heart of Jesus, I implore, that I may ever love thee more and more." Or if pressed for time, "My Jesus, mercy."

This was rote prayer such as J.D. Salinger resurrected in the "Jesus prayer" out of Holy Russia, with which he sprinkled his novel *Franny and Zooey*. The rosary is the same thing: repetition of prayers over and over while cogitating the "mysteries" (events) of Jesus' life and death.

All this contributed to acquiring a sense of the divine from one's earliest years, a habit of reminding yourself of God's presence. This was at the heart of Ignatian meditation. Placing oneself in God's presence (reminding yourself of his presence) was the first thing you did as you settled in for meditation. Psychologically, mentally, imaginatively, you focused on it, whether as a seventh-grader waiting in St. Catherine's middle aisle or a novice at his desk on a small, hard kneeler at 5:30 in the morning.

The Catholic-schooled among us took this for granted. Not all could do so. Among the brothers at Milford was a 40-ish swarthy, muscular little man of Middle Eastern ancestry who told me meditation did not come easy to him because he had not been trained in prayer by the sisters from his youngest days, as most of us novices had. He had gotten or absorbed lessons in antisemitism, however, and would let that slip out now and then while acting as straw boss for novices sent to help him clean up the men's retreat house on novitiate grounds.

Meanwhile, at Milford our first three days got us acclimated. Our cubicles, six to a dorm, had cot and small wardrobe and chest of drawers with white porcelain bowl on its top. We carried the bowl down the hall to the bathroom, filled it, brought it back, and shaved before a small mirror, cubicle curtains drawn, then took the soapy water back to the bathroom for emptying. Our pro tem "guardian angel" even showed us how to make a bed.

THE JOY OF SILENCE

We learned about "sacred" silence from 8:30 p.m.—preparation of points for next morning's meditation—to 7:15 breakfast after mass. After points came examination of conscience at 8:45, "examen" we called it, using the Latin word. "Points and examen" became as much a part of our lives as breakfast and dinner. We also were to speak only when necessary throughout the day, and then in Latin, except for recreation after lunch and dinner and on walks and at games.

On the fourth day, we went silent for a three-day retreat, a triduum. Even this minor effort at soul-searching was known to separate man from boy, sending the boy home to mother, father, and all things comfortable and familiar. The novice may have had no burning desire to be alone with his thoughts, but he had to try it out if he wanted the the black robe.

The cassock, that is. We were measured for it during the first few days. The brother tailor, a quiet man, friendly and peaceful-looking, had got the length and breadth of each of us, chest, neck, sleeves, height. Returning to the cubicle after points and examen of the third day of this short retreat, each found the cassock laid across his bed. It was a serviceable garment, without buttons, just a clasp at the neck. No monsignor would be caught dead in one. With it came the cincture, a sash maybe three inches wide, which you wrapped twice around your middle. Tuck it in, tied with a handy loop, and you were ready for the day.

There we were after our three days of silence and meditation with our new apparel, worn with a novice collar, not yet turned clerically backwards. We had completed the first probation, achieving full-fledged novice status. The second probation, the rest of novitiate,

COMPANY MAN • 15

was coming. The third would come much later, after ordination. But there were probations inside this probation—a month in the kitchen or refectory or outside keeping the grounds in shape or elsewhere.

BENDING THE KNEE

For now we were headed for life in a very slow lane. Early to bed, we were to meditate first thing in the morning for an hour and for a half hour every afternoon. Flexoria we called the latter, probably as in the flexor (bending) muscle. In this case we bent the knee to pray. It was a sort of late-afternoon spiritual pick-me-up.

There was a dietary pick-me-up too, "haustus," Latin for what's drunk or eaten. A snack? The haustus table would be set up at the end of the refectory, with coffee, milk, and (dry) bread. I arrived at Milford with no taste for coffee, much less a habit. Only later did I succumb, to stay awake in philosophy classes.

Another daily event was reading from *The Imitation of Christ*, by Thomas a Kempis, a 14th-century spiritual guidebook and Christian classic which promoted otherwordliness, as in exhorting the reader:

"For what would it profit us to know the whole Bible by heart and the principles of all the philosophers if we live without grace and the love of God? Vanity of vanities and all is vanity, except to love God and serve Him alone."

Another daily reading was in the three-volume "Rodriguez," thoughts on the spiritual life by a 17th-century Jesuit Alphonsus Rodriguez. This work, *Ejercicio de perfeccion y virtudes cristianas*, or *Exercise of Christian Perfection*, came in three well-thumbed green-bound volumes. The three were big and heavy, nothing to curl up with on a park bench. Rodriguez was full of stories. I especially remember those from Seneca, the Roman stoic philosopher, and early church writers with lurid tales of penance in the desert by hermits tormented by visions of beautiful women.

TWO SIDES OF THE HOUSE

We lived in a house divided, novices on one side, juniors on the other. We met only on "fusion" days, when both sides of the house gathered for meeting and greeting and softball or touch football. The latter honored the rule of "tactus" (never touch another, "even in jest") by requiring that you come no closer than a few inches of the opponent to down him. We called it passball.

In a few years we dispensed with that requirement, which was aimed primarily, I see now, at other touching than bowling over one's opponent on field or court, such as sliding and upending a third baseman. Indeed, I suffered such an indignity a few years later when a future Scripture scholar took me out at third. I flew, somersaulting on to my back but hanging on to the ball.

It was good clean fun, and believe me, for those who played, these games were a major, major recreational factor. Where some of us would have been without athletics can only be imagined. Indeed, my biggest distractions during novitiate meditation were not the girls I had left behind but the hits I made or double plays I pulled off or passes I caught—the stuff of consolation, to use a term from our lives of prayer—or strikeouts or balls dropped or double plays hit into—the stuff of desolation.

NO GIRLS ALLOWED

As for the girls left behind, I found it was mostly an out-of-sight-out-of-mind experience as long as we were sequestered in southern Ohio. A few years later, parachuted into Chicago for summer school at Loyola University only blocks from a beach, it was another story. The lovelies would walk by our dorm in their swim suits, their legs and rear ends sharp reminders of what we were passing up. I confided my feelings to the provincial in an annual conference. "They look pretty good, don't they?" said he, from which I rightly concluded that it wasn't going to get easy.

What I did not conclude was that, as I see it now, there was no middle way: stifle the impulse or die, or if not die, then at least have a deadly time of it trying to be a Jesuit, not to mention a nuisance to others, if not worse. Rodriguez with his tales of hermits in the desert attacked by devils in the shape of beautiful women was not far off the mark. To make this celibacy thing work, you had to close your eyes and grit your teeth, I have since concluded.

The novice master recommended angelic purity, and pretty much let it go at that, though "modesty of the eyes" (controlling what we looked at) was highly recommended and remains a worthwhile tactic, celibate or not. "A studied nonchalance," the master said. We were to resist temptation in thought and deed. No Jimmy Carter-like lusting in our hearts for us. It was a strategy that was to work for fewer and fewer of us as the years went by.

A TOUGH ROW TO HOE

In some ways the novitiate was a debilitating experience. An ex-Marine left, we heard, saying he'd never tried anything so hard. During the war, a non-citizen novice, probably a German or Italian national, was of at least nominal concern to the Feds, who asked that superiors keep an eye on him. Told he'd be checked on morning, noon, and night, as were we all to make sure each was at his desk meditating or examining his conscience, the agents protested: "Hey, we don't want you to hound the guy."

The life had its Spartan aspects. We washed and shaved in our cubicles, with cold water if we had filled our basins the night before, with hot if in the morning; it meant we had donned cassock for the trip down the hall. There was no padding down in a t-shirt. It was always the cassock except during manualia (chores) and games—gray jacket for the one, black for the other, almost a prison uniform, and out walking, where we dressed casually. Always wearing a shirt with collar, however, never a tee shirt.

First visit to the community chapel on the first floor was considered essential, as providing focus for our Blessed Sacrament-centered prayer lives. This "domestic" chapel was a beige-walled, businesslike place. The novice chapel, on an upper floor, was smaller, darker, more intimate. Both had altars, of course. In each a mass was said at 5:30, another at 6:00, another at 6:30, and there were other altars throughout the house, some stuck in an alcove at the end of a hall. Such was the overflow of priests—faculty, administration, retired, visiting. Each said mass alone, with single server, silently except for murmured responses. This was years before celebration of mass by two or more priests—"concelebration"—now taken for granted when two or more are gathered.

FOOD, GLORIOUS FOOD

The 6:30 community mass in the domestic chapel was attended by all novices but those who served mass elsewhere. The longest 15 minutes of the day were those between the end of mass and breakfast at 7:15. The time was devoted to post-mass "thanksgiving," each kneeling, wrapping up the morning's prayer, trying to strike motivational and/or consolatory paydirt after his hour of meditation and half hour of mass, but alas, too often straining for effect and trying not to think about breakfast.

Breakfast—more ample than probably any of us had experienced before our arrival at Milford—was a huge relief. Even in Lent, when menus were diversified so that you could eat less of a greater variety, it was up to you to hold back. One classmate of mine, determined and athletic, a bear for hard physical work when it offered itself, lost many pounds during his first Lent. But many of us gained weight in or out of Lent. We weren't eating on the fly or going out late and were leading good, clean lives.

Breakfast was silent. So were lunch and dinner most of the time, except for reading from the pulpit, as from a life of 19th-century Archbishop John Ireland or G.K. Chesterton. Dinner was at noon, farmer-style, when we arrived, but a few years later was moved to night. Reading was to supply food for the mind while eating, but also practice for juniors, the full-time students in their third and fourth years at Milford.

They read from a pulpit at one end of the dining room, without a microphone: the reader was learning to project and be heard. If he pronounced a word wrong, the speech teacher at the faculty table at the other end of the long room hollered, "Repetat!"—Latin for "Say it again!" The reader never knew when a "repetat" was coming. We novices sat and ate and listened, knowing that if we persevered, we too would one day stand in that pulpit trying to be heard by 200-plus eaters, never knowing when we'd be so peremptorily interrupted.

Not every meal was silent. On special days that averaged out to once a week or so, after a minute or so of reading, the rector at the faculty table would say "Tu autem, Domine, miserere nobis" ("Lord have mercy on us") and we would reply, "Deo gratias" ("Thanks be to God"); and the entire 200 of us would burst out talking. At meal's end, he would say "Satis" (enough), and we'd go immediately silent for the prayer of thanksgiving after meal.

THE DIRTY WORK

We novices waited table, washed dishes, set tables. A brother was in charge of the refectory and scullery, "triclinium" in Latin, where dishes and glasses and placeware were washed in super-sized machines and then dried by hand. Another was in charge of the kitchen, "culina" as in "culinary." He was the head cook. The kitchen had its own wash, for pots and pans; hence the epithet "pot-scrubber," used by the irritated in place of "son-of-a-bitch" and the like. It was not as harsh and fit in better with the dignified, even exalted role for which we were destined.

Each novice took a turn working full-time in the kitchen or triclinium or the "garden"—with the brother in charge of grounds maintenance— or on the working farm a few miles away which supplied us with milk and chickens. These were month-long "probations," during which we lived a brother's life.

Another probation, newly established in the early '50s, was at Bellarmine Hall, a men's retreat house in northwest Chicago suburban Barrington. Second-year novices, having completed the canon-law-required year spent entirely in the novitiate, went off in twos to wait tables, wash dishes, make beds, clean toilets, and the like. Getting there was an adventure. In the absence of expressways, you had to drive through city and suburban streets. The driver for my partner and me, a brother stationed at the retreat house, took a route from the train station through west suburban Oak Park.

I was thrilled to go down Washington Boulevard past Lombard Avenue, a half block from the family house. But I knew that was all we would do. There was not the slightest chance the driver would go even a block off his course, if only to drive down Lombard, much less stop to let me have even a short visit. Not for another three and a half years, five years after I'd left home, was I to darken its door and sit at its dining room table and eat and drink and enjoy good time with family. This was detachment from earthly delights. We didn't fool around.

The month in Barrington was a major change of pace, exhilarating if tiring. The priest in charge was a big redheaded guy of nervous intensity who gave me quite a message at the end of the month, telling me I'd turn out all right if I were as good as my father, whom he knew. That would have been a wonderful thing to hear if I didn't suspect he thought I was lazy or otherwise deficient. However, even if I were prone to calling out my superiors, which I was not, I could hardly object to his comment, even when I took it as a slam at me.

A word here about the two years of novitiate and the "canonical" first year. Jesuits' two-year requirement was unique. All other religious communities—orders, congregations—imposed only one, as required by the church. The Dominicans, for instance, at the time accepted novices no earlier than after two years of college and ordained them to the priesthood after seven years, for ordination at 27. Jesuits accepted candidates after high school, for ordination at 31, but with two years of training scheduled after that, for a delay of full-time priestly work to age 33.

STRATEGIC RETREAT

As for the retreat house, Bellarmine Hall welcomed 50 or 60 men a weekend for a Friday-to-Sunday "closed" retreat. That is, the retreatants were out in the country far from the madding crowds they were used to, and were expected to keep silent and show up for four or five group "conferences" a day for lecture-sermons by the retreat master. Years later, I was to be a retreat master at this very place. The men would file in and listen. The retreat master and one or two other priests who lived there would be available for individual conferences and, of course, confession.

My father had been going to Barrington since it opened a few years earlier. He had made retreats in St. Louis, where the Jesuits had "the White House," and before that at the Franciscans' retreat house in Mayslake, near Hillside, a western suburb. But the Mayslake retreats were loose affairs, with silence not observed and, as I heard, card games at night for those who were interested.

Not so among the Jesuits, whose retreats were serious refueling operations. My father took them very seriously. They satisfied a spiritual hunger for him, though he'd never have put it that way. He'd had two years of Catholic schooling, just before confirmation at 12 or 13, on the West Side, and two years or so at Chicago's Austin High before becoming an apprentice printer.

From Joe, the retreat-house cook, I got a chance to be like Jesus, taking it on the chin and smiling. Joe was a rough-hewn character who found me eminently unlikable and tore into me once for saying something along pacifist lines that sounded unduly idealistic to him. He practically tore my head off as I washed dishes, yelling in my ear about war never ending, always was, always will be, and there was nothing I could do about it.

Someone, probably a fellow novice, mentioned it to the novice master when we got back. The master asked me about it nervously and was relieved when I brushed it off as Joe's just not liking me, without reference to what Joe might do to the next novice he didn't like. The novice master apparently took it as a case of a novice's being willing to put up with shit. We weren't supposed to respond in kind and were supposed to rejoice in it for the sake of the kingdom and to be like Jesus.

On the other hand, he couldn't be matter-of-fact about this fellow at Barrington. He hadn't relished the idea of complaining about him to the priest in charge, though I'm sure he would have done so if necessary, and I can't say I blame him. I know I didn't blame him at the time. I was reshaping and steeling my soul and couldn't be bothered.

BIG NOT-EASY COMING

Return now to the first weeks of novitiate, inching by as we approached the Big Muddy, Big Ditch—name your obstacle course—the Long Retreat. We had arrived August 8, another group arrived on September 2. We and a few novice brothers, who had arrived one by one in the previous year on their own schedule, not in a class, were en route to a 30-day meditationfest that would end on the last Sunday of October, the feast of Christ the King, when we would emerge in all our glory, having survived a long initiation.

If it sounds grueling, consider the fraternity initiation I and one other of us had undergone at Loyola—six weeks of programmed humiliation and physical punishment that led us to brotherhood and in some cases lifelong friendship. Those were the days. Youth was wasted on the young, Shaw said, calling it a pity. Not so this coming novitiate event. Rather, it was to be life-changing.

The retreat would be the Spiritual Exercises of St. Ignatius Loyola, the 16th-century hidalgo with an itchy sword arm turned dedicated religionist. Disabled by a cannon shot in a siege of the Basque city of Pamplona in northern Spain, at 30, he underwent painful surgery for vanity's sake, so he could wear snappy boots. While recuperating, he ran out of inspiring stories of military derring-do and turned to lives of Jesus and the saints.

These inspired him in quite another direction. He began to reassess himself. From dreams of earthly glory he turned to heavenly. Accustomed to kingship as going concern, he pictured Jesus as his king, his beau ideal, his general. Two years after his wounding, he found himself in a cave at Manresa in northeastern Spain, fasting and doing penance and taking on noonday devils and all others that showed up.

He had a close call getting to Manresa. He ran into a Moor and discussed religion as they rode along. It was almost fatal for his newfound spiritual intentions and for the Moor, who spoke disrespectfully of the Blessed Mother. Ignatius had to think twice about that and came within a hair's breadth of chasing the fellow and sticking him with his dagger. The story, a good one, is that he left it to the mule, who took a different road, away from the Moor.

In the cave, wrestling with himself more than with devils for 10 months, not all of it in the cave, he was born again. He came from the experience a changed man. Not all of it in the cave, because he had to get out and do odd jobs for food, in which respect he was a sort of Thoreau at Walden Pond, but he did not eat as well.

Out of the 10 months also came a scheme of spiritual rebirth and renewal, the Spiritual Exercises, which in a few years took shape as a little book that shook the world, a sort of blueprint for self-examination and conversion. It was these exercises, all 30 days of them, to which we 50 young Americans gave ourselves in the month of October, 1950. Let us consider that experience.

DOWN TO BASICS

On the first day of the first week, we went at the meaning of life, rehearsing what we already had heard and absorbed, most of us, from our youngest days. It was simple stuff, reminiscent of the Baltimore Catechism: God made us, we are meant for his purposes. More precisely, "Man is created to praise, reverence, and serve God our Lord, and by this means to save his soul." Basic stuff, bread and butter Christianity, worth repeating. We heard it in conferences with "Father Master" in our little third-floor chapel, with its dark walls, dark kneelers, dark chairs. In the conferences he provided "points" for meditation. The schedule was "points and meditation" four times a day, with points for the morning given the night before, the better to fall asleep thinking about them, the better to wake up still thinking about them. It was an exercise in thought control. We were concentrating mightily.

Father Master was also "the master," as we commonly referred to him, without embarrassment at using a phrase from Eastern religious discipline, not even thinking about it. For one thing, he was in no way Eastern. He was Bernard "Bernie" Wernert from Toledo, Ohio. Gaunt, dark-complexioned, big-eyed, intense even when his face broke into lines with the broadest of smiles, he sat facing us at a little table on which he laid notes on typed half-sheets. He never looked unprepared and always seemed to say just what he intended.

We looked at that face four times a day for 30 days, minus three break days separating the "weeks" of the Exercises—divisions of meditation material rather than seven-day periods. We meditated also on break days but far less, being given the morning and afternoon for hiking and playing. The news of a break day came on the second-floor bulletin board after breakfast. The first of these was the tenth day, after nine days thinking about life and death. One of us, a high-strung track man who had special permission to go off running on his own to let off steam, burst out almost hysterically at the news.

DEATH'S STING

No wonder. After creation and our purpose in life on the first day, we heard about sin, death, hell, with a little bit of heaven tossed in at the end. We pictured ourselves on our death beds, kneeling with shades drawn and lights dimmed. The sun still shone outside or didn't, I can't remember. But I remember the meditation and recalled it years later, when I told a psychiatrist about it. He wasn't treating me. My wife and I were at dinner with others of his profession prior to a talk by the famous death-and-dying expert Elizabeth Kubler Ross. When talk with the professionals came to imagining oneself dying, it came to me: I had done that, in the First Week.

Into such a week, put your more than usually pious, relatively sensitive 18-year-old. Put him in a dark room and have him meditate on his death as if it were then and there, and you have the potential of a soul-searing experience—Billy Graham, who had his own life-changing episode, and John Wesley, founder of Methodism, would recognize it. I shrink from too dramatic a designation, but I do know that tossing hell into the mix in another of the first nine days—before or after, I do not recall—gives a young man pause.

It was certainly geared to help a back-sliding novice think twice about leaving the novitiate, "checking out," as we put it, or just "checking." Neither fear of ostracism on leaving—for most of us, there would have been none—nor precipitate ending of a chosen career (we were young enough to start over, so what?) nor a dipping of one's personal flag with accompanying sense of failure (again, so what at this stage?) did the job on the dark days of the 22 novitiate months yet to come. It was the fear of hell that hung in the minds and hearts of some of the weary and disconsolate.

So much for hell. The first week had heaven too. We pictured torment and loss in meditating the one and joy without end in the other. Even death had its light moments. Demonstrating how we know neither the day nor the hour, Father Master listed Jesuits he knew who had cashed in without a moment's notice. As he did so, Charley O., Marine vet and highly motivated spirituality practitioner, got a giggly fit, he said later. He kept it bottled in at the time, and many men together could not have spied it, I'm sure. It was the image of those Jesuits dropping like flies, he said later. Which goes to show, you can find a laugh in just about anything if you just let the spirit move you.

TRAVELING WITH JESUS

Break day done, we embarked on the second week, meditating on Jesus as itinerant preacher and miracle-worker. This was our introduction to the Ignatian imagination. We were put to picturing or contemplating Gospel events, as opposed to great and noble thoughts. In episode after episode, we imagined ourselves there with Jesus, almost without attention to the meaning of it for ourselves but rather to get familiar with him. This was a far cry from the moralizing Sunday sermon we had grown up on, staples of our upbringing: The boy Jesus found in the temple? Honor thy father and mother. The wedding feast at Cana? A word for the sacrament of matrimony. Multiplying the loaves and fishes? Consider the boy with the two loaves and how our little becomes a lot thanks to Jesus.

We had prayed to get things or win things or improve ourselves, as with "Jesus meek and humble of heart, make my heart like unto thine," a standard "aspiration," or short prayer, of our Catholic-schooled youth. This time we pretty much just looked at Jesus and the people in his life. Lessons were obvious enough, supplied by context, but they weren't the main thing. That was the scene itself. We practiced "application of the senses" in prayer, much as writing students learning how to see what others missed.

A few years later I did a paper on the poetry of Robert Southwell, one of the English Jesuits who was caught by Elizabethan priest-hunters and executed. Southwell's "Burning Babe" and other poems reflected his Spiritual Exercises experience, according to critics I consulted. I wrote to demonstrate that. Here we were more or less monks in a monastery, meditating the hours away to get closer to Jesus, and all the while imbibing a whole poetic vision or style. It was no simple thing being a Jesuit.

This second week, covering seven or eight more of the 30 days, was a breeze compared to that hell and death stuff. The shades stayed up, the sun came in, Father Master got light-hearted and tried humor at times. His points (for meditation, remember) were not aimed narrowly at inculcating a position on anything but rather at infusing a habit. We were gearing up for a life of prayer. But there was more.

CHANGING LIVES

We were also gearing up for a life-changing decision. Here in this second week, we ran into the element of the Exercises that one could argue is most peculiarly Ignatian. Ignatius had done a one-eighty, going from glory-seeking in the macho-chivalric mode of hair-trigger touchiness to ascetical stoicism mixed with tough-minded resolve. In the process he became a specialist in the life-changing decision. He had stumbled on it while recuperating and had gone to Manresa after deciding to change his life. So with us. We entered the novitiate after deciding to change ours. He took ten months to rub his nose in that decision. We had two years to do it, with emphasis on this 30 days. (Actually, we took our ten months in the 15th year of training, after theology, what was called tertianship, about which more later.)

So in this second week, we heard about Ignatius' three kinds of men, his exercise in being honest with yourself. The one kind, faced with the hard, noble thing to do, never quite decides. The second decides in a way that pleases him and deceives him at the same time. The third bites the bullet. We were to be the third kind of man: whatever we decided we should do, we would do, without ifs, ands, or buts. It's what real men did.

That said, the Second Week was a fooler. Relaxed we might be picturing Jesus touring Israel, doing miracles and preaching. But there were these Three Kinds of Men and before that, at week's start, the call to arms of "the earthly king," a what-if situation quickly converted to the call of the heavenly king, Christ. This was the sort of call that moved Ignatius and his fellows. Oh to have a king to whom one could pledge undying loyalty and unstinting service! Nay, there was such a king, and his name was Jesus Christ!

The king part didn't do much for us, but we did have service in mind or we wouldn't have been there. We meditated with a view to how it should affect our lives. In the midst of these travels with Jesus, we were asked what side we were on. Whose flag or standard would we follow, his or the devil's? In the Meditation on Two Standards, "the one of Christ, our Commander-in-chief and Lord; the other of Lucifer, mortal enemy of our human nature," it was Jesus or Satan. Life on earth was a warfare. This was boot training.

We were to embrace "spiritual," even actual poverty, "contumely and contempt," and what was to result from accepting it, humility. For us it was to be poverty not wealth, contempt not worldly acclaim, humility not pride. From this we were to proceed to "all the other virtues." We were not just to put up with trouble when it showed on our doorstep, we were to go looking for it.

BITING BULLETS

The Three Kinds of Men had to decide whether to keep a bundle of money—10,000 ducats, not stolen! The first and second kind of man wouldn't or couldn't give it up. The third got himself to the point where he didn't care. He was detached, ready to do justice to the important thing—to follow the king, ignoring the consequences. Once you got to this point and as long as you stayed there, you were ready for trouble.

There were moments of peace in this Second Week, the sort that comes when you relax and say let the chips fall, etc. But the pressure was building. There we were as young as seventeen, as old as the mid-30s, 50 of us, getting up at 5 a.m. in a Spartan dormitory and hitting our kneelers at 5:30 for a soul-searching session in the presence of God, pledging to do hard things. God and Christ wanted a few good men. Did we qualify? A few months short of 19 myself, about as raw as I could be, I overflowed with resolve. I was ready to storm the bastions, I told myself and whoever else was listening, in this case God the Father, Son, and Holy Ghost and all the saints and angels—plus the novice master when the occasion offered.

There was a third motivational meditation, or ploy, from the Ignatian playbook, about the three "modes" or degrees of humility, actually dedication. The first was readiness to do what's needed to be saved, "namely, that I so lower and so humble myself, as much as is possible to me, that in everything I obey the law of God." No Faustian bargains: "Even if they made me lord of all the created things in this world . . . for my own temporal life, I would not be in deliberation about breaking a Commandment, whether Divine or human, which binds me under mortal sin." I wouldn't even *think* about it.

Pledging the second degree, I wouldn't even think about a venial sin, "not for all creation, nor because they would take away my life." I was to care not about money or honor or how long I lived, as long as God was served and my soul was saved.

There was more. I was to choose a hard life to be like Christ, who was poor and was treated badly. This hard life was to be my preference. This was the background for meditating on the public life, to look at how Jesus lived and pledge ourselves to imitation. This was years before the "What would Jesus do?" business got traction.

If we used to just pray by asking for things or trying not to let things worry us, now we were to become absorbed completely. We may have said our morning and night prayers and gone to mass on Sunday and made a weekend retreat and considered ourselves pretty pious. Now we were in the big leagues. And we were just getting started.

WHIPS AND NAILS

We got to Palm Sunday in our meditations and then had a second break day, 17 or 18 days into the retreat. Now the Third Week, on the passion and death of Christ—Mel Gibson stuff, imagining it all in detail. When Gibson's movie came out, I was not tempted to see it and did not, having already spent a week immersed in the gruesome, tragic denouement. Shades were drawn again, mood turned somber, laughter disappeared, the novice master did not smile. For five or so days, we went chapter and verse, line by line through the grim tale.

We imagined details—whips, nails, betrayal, agony of prayer, submission to the will of the father, burlesque-like denial by Peter, the sorrows of the mother, the loyalty of the women friends. We knelt four times a day for 45 minutes at a time, after a half hour of listening to the master. If there was hell to deter the tempted, there was now also the idea of betraying our leader.

We saw Jesus in the garden of olives as bearing the sins of the world, ours included, which he was expiating. We saw ourselves as contributing to his suffering. Focusing on that, we prayed for forgiveness and pledged fidelity. Jesuits of that time engaged in such gut-wrenching. They would in various degrees adopt intellectuality—the philosophical mind was coming—but at the start they engaged their feelings to the utmost.

Meditating on passion and death with shades drawn, as we had on death and judgment, we inhabited a sort of spiritual steam room. Rising and praying, keeping silence all day, we would look forward to the conference, when we didn't have to work but could be talked to. The master was engaging. He sat at his little table, the soul of control and focus.

MASTER OF MEN

Apart from his role as retreat master, he was also there when you needed him. I knocked on his door once before the retreat, when I'd had a very bad day, had gotten tired out playing too much baseball on a sub-tropically hot and steamy day and trying too hard on various other things. I was played out and feeling very sorry for myself. Opening his office door, he took one look and knew I was careening toward trouble. His face softened visibly. "Carissime," he said, using the novice's title—Latin for "dearest," or even "dear friend"—not my first name as he usually did, "the Lord wants you here." He had read me perfectly, having probably seen dozens of faces like mine, strained and contorted. And he knew just what to say. I was stopped in my tracks by his combination of empathy and conviction. I stayed.

Staying was a big issue, to be sure. We were told not to doubt our vocation. Leaving was a very bad thing. This was underlined by procedure. Those who left the novitiate ("checked out" or just "checked") just disappeared. No notice was posted. The manuductor, a novice appointed as a sort of trusty who met daily with the master, would be informed. He had to know if someone was no longer available for various jobs, from dishwashing to helping in the garden. The word would get out, of course, if only from those in his dorm who saw an empty cubicle and knew no one had died or been stricken. Years later, leaving the Jesuits, I said goodbye to five or six contemporaries at a high school loading dock before driving away in my rental car for my first ex-Jesuit job. It was not like that in the 50s. You left in the dead of night or at least when almost no one was looking.

During the retreat the master was almost our entire contact with the world outside ourselves. He was a deeply conscientious man, intense but endowed in my opinion with adequate common sense.

He could shoot down excessive mortification plans with a wry look, so that the novice who was overly interested in saving on tooth paste or socks (ours was a small world with big goals) would think twice about it. He enjoyed life. The ready grin was not shown to make points; among his peers, he would sometimes laugh so hard he could hardly stop. He also could look very serious and stern without half trying. By and large, in my opinion, we were in good hands, though some resented him as harsh and out of touch.

Penance and mortification got closer than usual attention in the third week. As we contemplated suffering and death, we heard or read about "rules to be observed" as to eating and drinking. The one that stayed with me is the last, that in deciding how much to eat and drink, the time to decide is after a meal not before it. When you're fat and happy, you see things differently, of course. If you found you were giving in too often, then you were to eat even less. Go against yourself. In Latin that's "agere contra," to go against. It became a byword in Jesuit asceticism.

ALLELUIA TIME

We finished the week and had our break day—walking in the morning, playing "passball" in the afternoon (touch football without touching), returning to retreat mode with 4:30 "flexoria," afternoon meditation—and entered the Fourth Week, about the risen life of Christ. If you never thought four days of meditating could be fun, then you never did it after three-plus weeks raking over the coals in your soul including a long, hard look at suffering and death on a near-cosmic scale. Done was the crucifixion. It was full speed ahead to the resurrection.

Again we imagined and looked, applying our senses. "Contemplated" was the term. Now it was of Jesus risen, gospel accounts of appearances, including at a lakeside fish fry, on the walk to Emmaus, in the upper room, his followers amazed and heartened. Now the novice master found room for jokes. He gave us a look at the lighter side of the spiritual life. "This is the day that the Lord has made, let us be glad and rejoice therein!" was the governing quote. We were looking at the side of religion that consoled and encouraged, having looked while trying not to blink at the hard side that challenged and (ideally) inspired.

This week also had its Ignatian specials. The best was the "contemplation to attain divine love," or in Latin *contemplatio ad amorem*. On this contemplation we spent the 30th day, which served as a sort of decompression chamber. We walked outside and looked at the birds in the trees, the sky above, the sun and clouds and rain spattering on pavement. We felt the autumn breezes—it was late October in the Ohio Valley—watched leaves falling, kicked them away. I swear, the novitiate experience was as much nature appreciation as anything else. Ensconced in a far suburb on 99 acres, we took long walks down country roads and through woods, often to our working farm and its villa a few miles away. Most of us were city boys. The novitiate years, and for two more years the juniorate, were nature immersion.

We got our running start at seeing God in nature from this Ignatian "contemplatio," which was typically systematic and detailed. Two points Ignatius made right away: one, that love showed itself in deeds not words, and two, it's to be mutual. Them that has, gives. You share with the other. Not having to say you're sorry and hundreds of other definitions aside, the love Ignatius had in mind was doing and giving. We were to do more than talk a good game.

END GAME

We finished. Prayer the next morning was a distracted thing. By now we were trying to recapture the retreat's best moments, times of "consolation," as we called it. Its opposite, "desolation," both standard terms, was the devil trying to sidetrack us and/or God testing us. So in prayer you tried to stay on track with a dollop or so of consolation. The whole thing was a concentrated exercise in mind and emotion control. Stay calm, stay cool, pray hard, and you had it made.

After meditation, mass, then 15 minutes remaining in the chapel for "thanksgiving." Then at 7:15 the breakfast bell, filing out of chapel across hall, past napkin boxes to the long tables festively arranged. Then grace, then sitting down, getting settled. The reader began in the pulpit, kitchen doors banged open on either side of it. Then the rector's "Tu autem, Domine" and our "Deo Gratias," and out we burst with our first relatively uninhibited conversation, our first not with fellow retreatants and our first at any meal for 30 days. Chatter, chatter, eat, eat. At a suitable time, maybe 45 minutes, the rector again: "Satis." Enough. Talking stopped. Finish breakfast on your own, get across the hall for a short chapel visit. Back to one's dormitory and desk. And there a pile of letters, also the first in 30 days! Yahoo!

Dinner, at mid-day then, was talk time too. Come 2 pm or so, we had a "fusion" recreation, novices and juniors. Teams competed. There was a lot of standing around and meeting or getting to know people. At this fusion we met the juniors from the other side of the house, standing on the grassy novitiate playing field with a novices vs. juniors softball game in progress, meeting and greeting. Most of us had gone to Jesuit high schools, which served as feeder institutions, though all but four in our year had a year or more of college. Chief among these were Loyola-Chicago, Xavier-Cincinnati, Notre Dame, and John Carroll-Cleveland.

DIGGING IN

When the bell rang at 4 pm or so, we headed into the routine, for novices beginning with 4:30 meditation, flexoria, and picking up next day with "manualia" (as in manual work). This was our sweeping and mopping, helping with laundry, waiting table, washing dishes, working on the grounds, and other chores at least an hour a day. Novices to a great extent kept the place running.

We also worked at the nearby laymen's retreat house, waiting table, making beds, cleaning up. This was a tidy white cinder-block building on one corner of our 99 acres on the Little Miami River, to which the so-called Men of Milford came for spiritual refreshment from Cincinnati and its environs. "It's a long time between drinks," ruefully commented Charley O., a novice who later left because of headaches after setting a standard for sheer intensity of piety and demeanor.

Charley, 25 or so, two years of law school behind him, was a Marine veteran from the South Pacific and China at the close of WW2. He'd been part of a Marine contingent stationed in a major Chinese city when Mao's army was on the move and at one point stood with his buddies as a last bastion against the advancing horde, which would have swallowed them up in a quick gulp, but didn't.

Charley had a dramatic flair, and his account of Marines under pressure stayed with me, 18 and with no military experience. As a novice I drew him once as my "admonition partner," who once a week or so had the chance, nay, duty, to keep me posted on my peccadillos, as I had the duty to keep him posted. This sort of novitiate practice tried men's souls. Your goal had been to ignore what bothered you about a buddy of acquaintance. Now it was to call him on it.

We were a bad match. Charley with his gravitas was one to give me advice, you could argue. But I him? Where was I to come up with something to help Charley become a better novice? His remembered advice for me, in any case, was to go easy on scratching my crotch. Like any man wearing underwear, I had an itch now and then, but relieved it too obviously, Charley said. You see these guys standing around scratching, he reminded me, with crooked grin. You don't want to look like that. I sure did not, and learned to be more careful.

CHECKING UP ON EACH OTHER

We also had a group exercise in criticizing each other, the "exercitium modestiae"—an exercise in moderation, perhaps, or in restraint or discipline, intended to smooth off rough edges in personal behavior, though in practice it became an exercise in humiliation or, on the other hand, in being a good sport, hearing what others knew or thought about you—all that and more.

In it the entire novitiate, 90 or more of us, stood in a circle, with one of us *kneeling in the middle*. The master of novices sat at a small table at a break in the circle farthest from the door. This was in the atrium, or big meeting hall, where novices gathered regularly. For the "exercitium" we gathered to call down the novice of the week, taking turns at citing a failure of decorum, politesse, or rule observance. "Carissime talks during manualia." He laughs too loud. He doesn't laugh enough. He does this, he does that. He doesn't do this, etc.

No one was required to say anything, but many did, including some who now and then scored on the laugh meter, relieving the tension. "Carissime keeps saying, 'You know,' but we *don't know*," said a good-natured older fellow, a Hoosier, bringing down the house. Or of a lanky, loose-limbed novice who wore his cincture low, "Carissime wears too much of his cassock above his cincture." This was said by a country boy, a farmer, of a big-city boy, puncturing the latter's flamboyant front. The city boy lasted, by the way, the country boy didn't, returning many years later from a far-flung mission field and taking to himself a wife.

For those who, thanks to genetic and family endowments, took themselves least seriously, the exercise—kneeling in the middle and being talked about—was not a big problem. For others it was. For Tom W., an ex-Marine reservist, footballer, ferocious jazz pianist, handsome dude, it was very hard. He knelt there with reddening face, utterly embarrassed by the experience, which provided lesser lights the chance to peck at him. An exercise in humiliation indeed.

I took it in a sort of dazed stride, having bought into the whole program and being not one to criticize. One critic said I talked about the toilet a lot. He did not like my toilet jokes, a form of humor I had absorbed at my father's knee. Another noted a pursing of my lips, also derived from my father. The first heard no more toilet jokes from me: that was my revenge. The other? I don't know what happened. I suppose I no longer did that with my lips.

My most exasperating moment came when, having myself criticized another for talking a lot about others—he was a gossip—I was braced by him in one of those private admonition sessions. In the standard post mortem with the novice master, he had claimed he didn't know what I was talking about. The master had told him to ask me about it. Conceding nothing, he broke what I took to be the rules of the game that said, look, we're trying to make this thing work; just write me off if you don't buy my criticism. He didn't, pressing me. I never did use the word gossip, trying to make indirection do the job, and ended up the embarrassed one.

Years later, during a theology summer in Chicago, a Chicago social worker told a few of us who were working with him, "You guys are like Communists." He referred to our being ready to go anywhere, any time. We laughed, but years before that at Milford, eyes rolled when meal-time reading told about Chinese Communists making people submit to public accusation. We identified with that.

CALLING ONESELF OUT

For that matter, we also publicly accused ourselves, singly and almost always voluntarily, saying a "culpa"—Latin for "fault"— before the whole community at meal time. Above the clatter, before the reading began, while the reader waited or was stopped in his tracks by the speech teacher if he didn't, a novice or junior kneeling before the faculty table would intone, "Reverend fathers and dear brothers in Christ, I say unto you my culpa for all my faults and failings . . . "

"What now?" the new novice, hearing it for the first time, asked himself.

The self-accuser, kneeling in front of the rector, who sat looking out at the whole refectory, named his fault, "especially for sleeping during meditation" or "grumbling about the food" or "breaking tactus on the playing field" or something else for which the offender was heartily sorry. The culpa-taker had two options. He could kneel with arms outstretched during grace, which took a while, being no simple "Bless us, O Lord," etc. but a sort of litany, in Latin, to which all responded. In which case he had grace after meal to look forward to, when he would repeat the kneeling-arms exercise, this time next to his chair. The other option was to rise after saying his culpa and head for a table of his peers, get back down on his knees, bend over, find a shoe, and kiss it! Yuck.

I did it both ways, and for the life of me cannot say which I'd recommend.

These culpas were the voluntary kind, decided on in the privacy of one's prayer or while mulling the day's events in the examination of conscience, the examen. You told no one ahead of time if you intended to take a culpa, though there was also the "pin culpa," imposed or pinned on the offender by a superior, as the minister of the house, its nominal disciplinarian, for something moderately egregious, like smuggling beer or leaving the campus in unauthorized fashion. The bad part about a pin culpa is that it wasn't the offender's idea. The good part was that it involved neither outstretched arms nor kissed feet, merely the humiliation, which wasn't much, to be honest. Pin culpas were rare.

But not the acts of penance, among which were the discipline and the chain. The former was a little whip, a cat of three tails, corded in a special machine in the basement by the brother who also did the house laundry, chattering endlessly the while. He was Tom Duris, as in the Latin for "so hard," *tam durus*. Tom worked his head off and kept us in clean underwear.

Using the discipline, you took your shirt off and swung the tails over a shoulder, stinging the skin. We did it in unison, in our cubicles with curtains drawn, at a signal from the one of us—slapping the mattress with the whip to start and slapping it again some seconds later to stop. With any luck the slapper made it a short count of, say, five seconds. This was at night before going to bed. Just the thing for a nightcap. We did it on Fridays during "regular order," which meant not in the summer or at holiday time such as Christmas or Easter. In Lent we did it also on Mondays and Wednesdays.

The chain, also a Brother Duris product, was a wire belt with wire ends turned inward. Not sharpened and not quite painful when held against the skin, but irritating. Tightened too tight was obviously asking for trouble, too loose led to rubbing back and forth on your epidermis. You wore the chain, or belt, on selected days in the morning, from arising at five to 7:10, when post-communion thanksgiving was cut short so that we could retire to our cubicles to take the damn thing off. In your cubicle, you disposed of it in your bottom drawer. And you know, it felt good to get it off. Breakfast tasted especially good on those days.

We were advised not to inform our parents of the practice. But then a book, *Obedient Men*, came out, by an English ex-Jesuit, Denis Meadows, spilling the beans about our penitential practices, about which mum was to be the word, said Father Master. When my parents brought it up on a visit, I got vague on the point, and they let it go. The whip and the belt were to be our little secret.

Among us, Peter Fox, from Indianapolis, had the answer to the discipline problem. Excited about it? Worried? "Keep your shirt on," he advised.

We don't know if he or anyone else did that. In any case, the practice survived probably for few if any once we left Milford and dormitory living. We know this about Pete Fox, that he handled his own case of polio, contracted in our first year at Baden, with amazing gracefulness. More later about the estimable Pete Fox.

LEAVING THE DESERT

It all sounds bad. But these exercises in humility, or humiliation, imposed or otherwise, did not crush us. In due time, most of us finished our two years, twice the canonical requirement, and if approved took our vows and went to the other side of the house. Gone was "carissime"—what we had to call each other. We would be now on a first-name basis with each other. We got a biretta, a four-cornered hat with wing-like handles on three corners that gave us a very clerical look, and a turned-around clerical collar.

We graduated from novitiate regulation to juniorate deregulation. No more afternoon meditation or manualia. No more reading Rodriguez with his tales of the desert. Far less introspection. The time spent on that would go to study. No more walking only in threes; now we could go in pairs. No more a million things that made up the relentless testing or annoyance. It was time to shed the chrysalis, straighten up and fly right into the world of literature. None too soon.

CHAPTER 2. LANGUAGE TRAINING: JUNIORATE, 1952–54

The glory that was Greece . . . the grandeur that was Rome.
—Edgar Allen Poe

As novices we answered to God alone. As juniors we also had teachers to worry about. We had studied God and ourselves for two years, praying up a storm. Now we studied Latin, Greek, and English literature, with a touch of history and public speaking.

The speaking part was not new. As novices we were nudged along in various ways. We addressed each other in small groups and eventually took our turn reading to a refectory-full of Jesuits during a meal. We each gave a "Marianum," also during a meal. This was a sort of narrative sermon connected in some way with the mother of Jesus. Mine was about a Jesuit in Mexico. I remember the word "Taramuhara," the name of an Indian tribe among which the Jesuit worked. We wrote the Marianum from scratch and delivered it from memory. I practiced mine in various places, including in the big musty attic, to an audience of trunks and crates.

My doing so was no small achievement. I had been advised to delay applying to enter the society—of Jesus, the Jesuits—directly from high school. The issue was my stuttering. If I were turned down for stuttering, Father Mahoney, the applicant "examiner," told me in an initial interview, it would be that much harder to get in on a second try. I ought to wait a year, he said.

THE MOTHER AND THE FATHER

I took the "L" home to Oak Park, from the North Side Loyola campus, and told my parents. My father objected, but I cut him short, standing at the foot of their bed, where they were reading and talking. I said I would wait. I had never before acted with such assurance in opposition to him. He accepted it immediately. It was my decision, one that partook of the privilege attached to the role I intended to fill. At 17 I was making a life choice that was reserved to me, and parents had to step back. We all three knew this.

These parents were exemplary in this matter. Once in the middle of the following busy year at Loyola, my father came back to my bedroom as I knelt saying my prayers before sleep. I was at Loyola and not DePaul, where I'd gotten a scholarship, because he had called the Loyola dean, a family friend, and told him, "You're going to lose this guy if you don't watch out." How's that for running interference?

The dean had talked to the president, another friend, and I had my Loyola scholarship. So my father had gone to bat for me with the understanding that I'd be entering the Jesuits some day. But his word this night, as I looked up from my prayers, was that if I didn't want to do it, I should feel free not to. Thing is, I did want to do it and almost never wavered in the midst of a great year with new friends. Such was my vision. I looked forward to Milford.

That parental bedroom, with its twin beds smack up against each other, was a comfortable night-time gathering place for me and my sister, 20 months younger. The three brothers had left the house in the previous two years, two to get married and one to enter Milford. They were war veterans. One had been a prisoner of the Germans. Another had served in France and Belgium. The one at Milford, the oldest, had mucked around the South Pacific as co-commander of a 12-man amphibious landing craft that happily never was used in a landing.

I have often recalled the laughter at my very funny father walking past one of the high bed posts and catching his suspender on it. I also have recalled my mother lying with hand over forehead, palm up, waiting out a headache of an afternoon, rosary in hand. But she would be part of the fun at night, as when we two had finished homework and hung about. My brothers too, when they'd been around.

I'd been a stutterer since before I started any kind of school, but not since I started talking, I was told. I managed well enough in school and elsewhere. Indeed, in high school I was "notorious" for raising my hand in class and having my say, I heard from my senior year religion teacher, Father Regan, shortly before I left for Milford. The impulse to have my say was stronger than any hesitation I had at getting stuck. Still is.

I don't know how my stuttering started: my first speaking had shown no sign of it. Trauma? None is recorded by me or anyone else. Delicately balanced psyche violated by the rush of life? Sounds good for whatever has ailed me in 80 years. The strong personality of a father? Strong but not overbearing presence: his memory delights me and has taken over quite a bit more for me than that of my mother, a lovely, lovable woman. Our kids once asked why I spoke of him more than her. It hadn't occurred to me. One thing: I identified with him.

So it goes, I suppose, with the father-mother contrast. It's probably good for a man to remember parents that way, as I do: the father strong if sometimes impulsive, the mother a softening influence. She could say, "That's not so good" about something I did, and it would stick. She was petite and pretty. My father was handsome, outgoing, prone to anger, as a young man not above knocking a man down if the occasion called for it. He and I saw a man once on a Loop street cowering while another smacked him. At the sobering sight, my father, not big on direct advice, quite soberly told me I should never let anyone do that to me.

Neither parent was soft. Both had requirements, if different ways to enforce or reinforce them. As a pre-schooler I once told my mother my feelings were hurt from something she had said. Forget it, she said, or words to that effect. When I entered the novitiate, a friend predicted it would be easy for me, because I was already leading a disciplined life. Not quite, but he had a point.

STUTTER-STEPPING

However it happened, by the middle grades if not sooner, I was a confirmed stutterer. As a seventh-grader I went for speech-therapy sessions with the Fenwick High principal six blocks down Washington Boulevard from our house. We sat weekly for an hour or so, he taking me through reading in a relaxed setting (his office) and thus giving me the experience of speaking smoothly.

I began to get better without realizing it. The principal, Father Van Rooy, a man of deep and commanding voice and presence, knew our family from the two years my brother Jake had gone to Fenwick. He had heard about me from my father, maybe at Fathers Club meetings. He did it for nothing, possibly in gratitude for what my father was doing for the school by way of publicity and thus fund-raising advice, certainly from a general desire to help a young lad and future Fenwick student. My parents had jumped into the fathers and mothers clubs, as they had also at St. Philip High on the West Side, when my brothers were students there, and at Loyola University, which each of the three had attended before going to war.

They were joiners, uninterested in bowling alone as discussed in the book of that title about the end of neighborliness in American life. In the high school clubs and parish activities, they often were with people they had grown up with on the West Side, where they had been teen-agers and young adults in the Austin neighborhood just east of Oak Park. Later, as a Fenwick student, I had instant identity with many who knew Jake, six school years ahead of me. As a seventh-grader with Father Van Rooy, I was someone to care about.

He took me through my paces, advising me to breathe easily and to speak on the outpouring of breath. His advice in the matter was like that of the professional clinicians at Northwestern University, to whom I went weekly during high school and in my year of college before entering the Jesuits. Whatever Father Van Rooy did, I began to get better. Catching me in advance of adolescent self-awareness, he got results without my even being much aware of it.

This was when I was still an unconscious stutterer, before I knew I stuttered in the sense that I took it into consideration before I spoke. That happened with adolescence, which made its conventionally tumultuous arrival in the next year or so, like a thief in the night.

Father Van Rooy was getting results, but I was under some sort of stress that piled up one night and brought on tears as I sat in the living room with my mother and father. For some reason I identified my time with him as something that had to go—it was an inconvenience—and I talked my parents out of requiring me to make the weekly six-block walk. My father called him and begged off. Some time later, one of my St. Catherine (grade school) classmates noted that I'd been getting better at my speech. And I hadn't even known it.

By the time I entered Fenwick, I had backslid. In freshman speech class—five days a week for every freshman—I stood on one occasion for the 15 seconds or so that seemed eternal, trying to say something. I finally got it out and continued with my account. The teacher, Father Conley, had waited me out. After class he asked if I'd rather not be required to give any more speeches. I said I'd rather give them. I was "notorious" for speaking out even if it meant stuttering, I noted earlier. I can only say the urge to do that conquered all.

At Milford things went pretty well until, after the Long Retreat, which left me worn out, my stuttering took on new life. There I was, in the order which had taken me in when I had controlled the stuttering, now back to stuttering. The close of the 30-day retreat had produced exhiliration but had not repaired nerve endings. The novice master caught it right away. We discussed it. I told him about my Northwestern experience—the controlled breathing, speech as vocalized breathing, the counting as key exercise: one, one-two, one-two-three, etc.—the trick was to control the breathing, using it all up no matter the count.

We decided I could use a partner to practice with, a fellow novice who would catch on to the theory and be a sort of sounding board. Later, at the urging of the "socius," or assistant novice master, Father John Wenzel, I described the process in writing. The master's name was Wernert, which gave us Irishmen and others Wernert and Wenzel, our one-two Germanic punch.

Father Wenzel was equally outgoing but more emotive and full of feeling than Father Wernert and appeared to lack his resiliency. He gave no hint of being distracted from his work, but now and then discussed possibilities of other employment, elsewhere than at the novitiate. It was impossible to imagine Wernert, an older man, giving expression to such an interest to a novice, or for that matter to anyone else.

Father Wernert found the man to help me, a Cincinnatian named Don Hogan who had commented on my Chicago accent on the first full day at Milford. "I like your accent," he said at table. "*My* accent?" I thought, wondering how he thought he sounded.

Hogan was perfect—sharp, personable, sensible, and an excellent shortstop, by the way, a veteran of Knothole League play in Cincinnati. He and I met every few days in a small mass chapel. I did the one, one-two business with him. But mostly I relaxed and got better at speaking. Hogan was a big help. Similarly, I was a help for Al Kezys, a classmate who had arrived from Lithuania knowing very little English. Al and I sat in that little room a half hour at a time, he trying English and I hearing him out, until he got very good at it. We were brothers helped by brothers, and took it for granted that it would be so.

HITTING BOOKS

Well ahead of juniorate time, I was doing quite nicely in the speech category and was ready to take my turn at meal-time reading, play-acting, debating, and the rest. Stuttering had ceased to be an issue. In any event, juniorate was study time. The dean greeted us the first day with a jocular nod to our apprehension at returning to full-time study. "We got you now!" he told us in an orientation session.

He himself taught us Cicero the essayist on friendship, "De Amicitia." Later we studied Cicero the orator, inveighing against the conspirator Catiline, "Quousque tandem abutere, Catilina, patientia nostra?" or roughly, "How long will we have to put up with you, Catiline?"

We had Greek from one of two Hartman brothers, both Jesuit priests. This one was big and broad-shouldered, a barrel-chested guy of somewhat arch demeanor who had studied at Oxford. His name was Ed and he became "Physical Ed." For him we put the Gettysburg Address into Attic Greek. It was a purely liberal pursuit, of no practical use whatever, he assured us, heading off narrow pragmatists' objections with which he had obviously grown bored. It was keen mental exercise, part of our ongoing enterprise of becoming aware of language and its contents.

We composed in Greek, and each year on the feast of the "golden-mouthed" fourth-and-fifth-century preacher John Chrysostom, one of Ed's students stood in the refectory pulpit and gave a sermon in Greek of his own devising. I have to ask you readers: How many of you have eaten lunch to such an accompaniment?

Our English teacher was Illinois-small-town-originated, a jokester who made so much of writing for publication that this junior had gotten his first check from a magazine before the two years were up. This man later became rector of the house and oversaw digging of a small lake at the juniors' "villa" a few miles' walk from the novitiate grounds.

Another English teacher, a kindly old fellow on his last legs, put us to reading essays and speeches and the like. He gave us a dose of pure style, much of it 19th-century stuff, British and American, which as a reading preference has remained with me, I must confess. A sweet guy, if not with a lot to say, he once crashed to the pavement before my very eyes. I wasn't kidding about last legs. His illness, whatever it was, did him in a few years later.

The speech teacher doubled as a history teacher. The history course was a holding action, so involved were we in literature. Public speaking, on the other hand, was front and center for us as future teachers and preachers, as I have said. This was William F. Ryan, as strong a personality as we ran into in those days. He wore thick-lensed glasses, was pudgy and had a look of softness about him.

He had a pleasant idiosyncrasy, clipping the New York Times in various subjects for various juniors' reading. Once I had taken on play-directing, under his rather distant moderation, my clips were about drama. He'd drop them on my dormitory desk, and there I was checking out Brooks Atkinson and others in the nation's newspaper, something I probably wouldn't have been doing if I'd stayed home in Oak Park.

Willie F. (later I served with a Willie P.) Ryan's soft appearance contrasted mightily with his booming voice which he let loose during meals in his capacity of supervisor of reading. The word was "Repetat!"—Latin for "Repeat it" or "Say it again." It was our version of Sam's order to play it again in "Casablanca," but without the dreaminess. His repetat cut through the dining room clatter— may I say it? like a not knife through soft butter?—stopping the reader in his tracks.

Sometimes he supplied the correction, as "roof" with the long "oo" versus short "uh." The Irish setter who roamed the grounds was Rufus, and the legend was that Father Willie's repeated "roof, roof" elicited a bark from Rufus, who heard it through the open refectory window on a summer day. One of many good stories that floated among us.

Willie Ryan looked soft and flabby, but he wasn't soft. On the day he'd had a tooth pulled, he did not give himself the day off but sat in the rear of his juniorate classroom spitting blood into a cup while student speakers performed. Later, at Loyola Academy–Wilmette, Illinois, he ruled his senior English classes with strong personality, booming voice, and strict requirements.

In the juniorate he also ran – as I said, from a distance – the drama program, two plays a year, on November 13, St. Stanislaus Day, when a three-act, full-scale production was staged, and in February, on so-called Rector's Day, when a shorter play was done. Both were one-night stands to a full house, including the entertainment-starved novices. I appeared in two of these and directed a third, the St. Stanislaus Day performance in my second year.

The saint in question, patron of novices, was Stanislaus Kostka, the 16th-century Pole who had not even made it through novitiate before dying in the odor of sanctity. Novices had him as their model. Many years later, I stopped my Chicago Daily News coworker, columnist Mike Royko, in mid-gibe with this information. Royko had a sort of old-world skepticism and sometimes antagonism toward the church and was thoroughly identified as Polish, if only through his creation and alter ego, Slats Grobnik.

He was needling me one day about religion, and I scored one of the best conversational hits of my life by telling him about the Pole St. Stanislaus as my model of how to live for my two years as a novice. "Really?" he said, abandoning his gibe of the moment and walking back to his corner office apparently impressed.

As juniors, we had a Belgian for our model, St. John Berchmans. From his life you could figure out the Jesuit rules, we were told, so assiduously did he observe them, including his badgering a teacher until he, Berchmans, understood the day's lesson. Never in my life was I to know or meet a Belgian columnist with whom to make a similar point, however.

In any case, let us praise Willie F. (for Fortune, a family name) Ryan, that least athletic of men, for putting muscle into the speech and speech patterns of us juniors. "If words *mean* anything," he would rage against the dying of light shed by precise expression, strongly urging us to say it right.

DEAN'S LIST

John A. (Gus) McGrail, the dean, on the other hand, never raged. Short and stocky, an athlete in his time, he was the soul of precision, encouragement, and good humor. If we were to yawn, he once advised, we should do it so that "many men together" would not know it. Faced with a difficult task, we should keep in mind that "what man has done, man can do." Most of all, he taught Cicero as if it was worthwhile in itself.

This is noteworthy. We were coming from a spiritual hothouse, where we had investigated ourselves unrelentingly, applying rules and spiritual advice in daily meditation. Now we were to look outward, at Cicero, Virgil, Homer, Thucydides, Shakespeare, Milton. One summer I read "Paradise Lost" out loud, alone, reveling in the cadences. We memorized Greek drama and acted it out on a small stage. We did the same for Shakespeare. We declaimed Cicero. We took secular, pre-Christian learning seriously. It was new for us. Not even in our pre-Jesuit Catholic classrooms had we so obviously embraced such material. It's as if we were big boys now, able to to see beauty bare, to adapt Euclid per Edna Millay.

Such experience had as much to do with making us Jesuits as the Long Retreat. We were to think and react with a view to the best thinkers in Western tradition. Years later I was chided by a Chicago monsignor for sending our kids to non-Catholic colleges. "What about your tradition?" he scolded, signalling the tongue-wagging and head-shaking or -scratching that had been a silent chorus to my wife's and my decision, or rather, our children's decisions. But he and I did not look to quite the same tradition, I decided. His was Catholic-no-matter-what, mine was Catholic as part of and crucial to Western civilization. So off our children went, to Vassar, Swarthmore, Carleton and the like, as part of their affirmative action program, I have thought, sprinkling Irish Catholics in their midst.

Not all Jesuits bought into this heavy-learning business. "Are you an intellectual?" a Chicago-based Jesuit asked me playfully in my father's presence during a visit to Milford during my juniorate. "I'm working on it," I said, adding, "If so, what can I do for you?" His was the skeptical, I might say utilitarian mentality, he a friendly, gregarious man whom my parents knew from their Loyola University parents' experience.

Much later, a colleague on the Xavier University faculty took strong exception to my joining a protest of treatment by police of anti-war protesters and my reporting of it in the Province Chronicle. Our discussion ranged beyond that far enough somehow for me to invoke John McGrail's juniorate teaching about the validity of the purely secular. Fair enough, but I didn't have to tell the fellow he was full of shit, now did I? I sure didn't learn that at Father McGrail's knee, and even less from Ignatius's rules for conversation with an adversary.

On another occasion, the minister of the Milford house—in charge of running it in all things material—equally affable and friendly, wryly spoke of those who got impractical about daily life, aiming especially at spenders-without-common-sense. He considered it important to make this well-aimed, wholly legitimate point with us as a group, but conversationally with a few of us he demonstrated amused scepticism at my grand scheme, as I recall it, of comparing the Roman historian Tacitus to Hemingway—which I never got around to doing, by the way. Nor had anyone else, I was reasonably convinced, until, by heaven, I found just such a comparison in a review on Amazon of a Tacitus translation whose lack of "redundant verbiage" provided "a curious parallel" to Hemingway. I'll be darned.

WRESTLING WITH LANGUAGE

Indeed, not all of us bought into the literature and, later, philosophy study in which we were immersed for five years in all. How could this not be so? None of us came from scholarly families that I can recall. Indeed, one mother, an articulate, competent woman, fearing a supposed distancing from real people, told her son not to get a doctorate. He did, much later, in theology. But she had made an exception for theology. We were absorbing the concept of "the hyphenated priest"—priest-scientist, priest-editor, and the like, especially, of course, priest-teacher, with whatever studies any of it would require. But not all our parents were ready for it.

The fathers came to visit Milford—printers, salesmen, ground traffic controllers, fire engine drivers, office managers. They were hard-working, not always gentle folk. A contemporary of mine who later got a (non-theology) doctorate told of being smacked with a folded newspaper at table one night when he complained about the food. Another told of his physician father, returned from World War II service, pushing people off the sidewalk as expression of his hard-gained hostility to the world.

My father had left Austin High School on the West Side of Chicago after two years to enter the printing trade. He had been a printing broker *cum* creative direct-mail ad man and producer of industrial catalogues for many years before I entered the society. He and my mother had been quite demanding in terms of doing well at school, leading me on one occasion to complain that some kids got praised for passing, but I got bawled out for getting B's.

None of it mattered in the juniorate. Like it or not, you got Latin, Greek, and Shakespeare. And speech training and speech experience. You read aloud, without a microphone, to 200 people busy eating and waiting table. You wrote and memorized and delivered sermons to the same eaters and waiters. You gave talks of every kind to your classmates. Willie Ryan threw his repetats into the refectory air, you caught them. And if you fumbled, you got a second repetat immediately, and a third, until Willie corrected you loudly and directly, telling you in front of all what the problem was. Words meant something. You had to get it right, you had to say it right.

For Jesuit high school graduates, Latin and Greek study was more of the same. From my non-Jesuit school and my year at Loyola I had excellent Latin but no Greek. The Latin we got now was Livy the historian, Cicero as essayist and orator, Virgil (including my third run through the 6th book of the Aeneid, the first in high school,the second at Loyola), Tacitus (another historian), Horace the poet, and maybe others whom I cannot recall.

The Greek was Homer, Thucydides the historian, the dramatists Sophocles and Euripides, and others. I memorized and delivered with feeling a speech from Sophocles on stage. And got ribbed for it. In Latin I could sight-read Virgil. Greek I could read aloud without a pause and get much of it on the run.

We were taught to hold Latin- and Greek-English desk dictionaries in mild contempt and instead used the big Liddell and Scott on a stand in the library, tracing words and phrases down to their beginnings. Willie Ryan's emotion-laden "If words *mean* anything!" was reinforced by our immersion in language. Later, in philosophy, we would hear about English "adversaries" to our scholastic positions who emphasized language analysis, as opposed to our leaning on essence and existence. In the juniorate we worked towards fluency in such analysis.

Along the way, I found myself challenged by Greek. Having none, I entered the beginner's class, but in due time got promoted. By the second year, I was in the A-class, reading the orator Demosthenes, and here I chickened out. I went to the teacher, Ed Hartman, and begged to be excused. Things were causing me pressure, I told him. "Well, 'things' are 'things,' aren't they?" he responded pointedly, not pleased at losing a student. Abashed, I agreed and let it go at that.

It was taking an easy way out. For all his rather grand manner, Physical Ed was worth sweating for. He was sharp but no bully. Neither was Willie Ryan. None of the juniorate teachers were. In fact, it was for me all in all a happy time. We were in the meatiest of study arenas, in my view. Books, poetry, language work, an emphasis on writing, including for publication, dramatics, including for me performing and directing plays, and lots of baseball, softball, touch football, even a little basketball, swimming in our own pool, hiking, picnicking, and talking, talking, talking.

Milford was an exurb, a nice middle American small town. Our walks could take us through Indian Hills, a posh 'burb, or past a golf course. The hills and woods were rural. In fact, we had a working farm in walking distance, complete with milk cows and chickens.

The farm had a "villa" in its middle where we gathered weekly for a day-trip walk destination and spent two weeks in the summer. After we left, Paul Allen as rector had a swimming hole put in. Pretty relaxing for the most part. We had neither beer nor babes to distract us from God, nature, and each other.

The novitiate-juniorate grounds proper` were a garden spot, full of athletic fields on either side of the three-story building, which had a pleasant design to it. There were big leafy trees, statues and shrines, heavy wooden chairs to flop into with a book. The Little Miami River flowed by on one side of the property, beneath a bluff. We skated and played hockey on the river now and then.

On the other side of the property was a cemetery where Father Zurlinden, known as "Zoo," walked *chanting* his divine office, his long hair pulled from behind over the top of his bald pate. He was a survivor of the Belize hurricane of 1931, in which nine Jesuits died. Their names appeared in the "necrology," or calendar list of the dead, on the anniversary of their perishing, to be prayed for on that day. Not just remembered, but prayed for: we wanted to spring their souls from the purgatory that awaited us all.

These were in large part two years among the lotus-eaters, like Ulysses on his way home, though come to think of it, we never did the Odyssey at Milford, just the Iliad.

PUTTING IT IN WRITING

It was the Sterling, Illinois, native Paul Allen who encouraged writing for publication. Easy-going in manner but assertive, he later became rector at Milford. He clearly enjoyed his work and us. His English classes were idiosyncratic exercises in reading and writing. I don't remember them for any depth of learning, nor did I do especially well in them or feel successful. But he emphasized the need to be concrete, partly out of concern for our airy-nonsense proclivities as young men immured in abstraction.

Our meditations on Jesus may have called imagination into play. But we were full of our goals and aspirations, and in much danger of boring people with generalities. He urged us to be sensible, that is, use our senses, telling what we saw, heard, etc. We did exercises in that. Years later I heard from a fellow newsman of the fiction writer Richard Sullivan, a favorite in those days, having his students do this at Notre Dame, even to describing the palms of their hands.

Paul Allen made so much of this that Ed Hartman, blessed with a finer mind than he and not the down-home boy that Paul was, felt obliged at one point in his Demosthenes class to make the point that we depended on abstraction to make our points; there was more to life and thought than sense impressions. It was a well-aimed corrective. But Allen's pushing us to get published was also well aimed. I took his advice and sent things out and sold them. My first check was for $8. It arrived from Franciscan Message, one of dozens of small Catholic publications that thrived in the '50s.

I wrote about Salazar, dictator of Portugal, as an example of enlightened leadership. As I told Chicago Reader columnist Michael Miner, forty-some years later, I wrote about Salazar knowing nothing about him, only what I picked up in an encyclopedia or a few articles in other magazines. But I could tell it intelligibly to an editor, who was glad to have my 1,000 or so words. It was the launching of a career, my friends.

It might not have happened if Paul Allen had not talked up the idea, or at least not soon. He instructed us in the mechanics, as to include self-addressed, stamped envelope (SASE), identify oneself briefly and clearly, etc., and telling us to keep it simple. I heard it later as the KISS rule, Keep It Simple, Stupid. Seen this way, it was the only kissing we were allowed, except for the crucifix on Good Friday.

This sending out of "fact articles" became a nice also-ran to my pursuit of language and languages. The joy of sale was not to be compared to spiritual consolation of a great meditation. But this spiritual consolation was happening less and less as the sometimes happy mists of novitiate prayer receded. I was losing my novitiate fervor, turning it in for something else, yet to be determined.

ON THE BOARDS

Meanwhile, there was play-acting. We did one-night stands for "the community"—novices, brothers, faculty, juniors. I played an energetic juror in a hubbub. Told to murmur "rhubarb" over and over as one of a group making indistinguishable murmuring, I gave it all I had, and my "rhubarb" was overly distinguishable. Still, I was in there trying, and Ludwig Stiller, from a small Indiana town and eventually of Nepal as a missionary, liked my energy and cast me in a corny one-acter about a hard-of-hearing man, "What's That You Say?" The play began with me on the stage, alone, saying nothing, trying to catch a fly.

There didn't have to be a real fly, I realized early into rehearsals. Where would we get one we could train? There may have been some sound-effect buzzing, I don't recall, like the shaking of metal foil for a thunder effect later for "George Washington Slept Here." There certainly was some high-level histrionics on-stage by me, as I held forth for two minutes, running about with much gesticulation and silent-film-style grimace. Dear Reader, they liked me, offering up heartfelt laughter. At that moment, it was push me out the door and send me to Improv Theater; I was ready.

But of course, hours later I was at my desk on my knees, the sun not yet risen, declaring my nothingness before God. Besides, there was Cicero to consider. "O tempora, O mores" and all that, not to mention St. John Berchmans' oft-repeated "Quid hoc ad eternitatem?"— What's this got to do with my life after death?

The big boost to my brief and glorious theatrical career came some months later when I got the director's job for the St. Stanislaus Day performance on November 13, that young Pole's feast day. This was the day novices were relieved of household tasks (manualia), and juniors took over. Juniors also put on a play. The dean picked me to direct it. I had my choice of a first-year junior as assistant director. Charley Law was just fine. We had been honors-course classmates at Loyola and were friends. He was a big fellow, with a built-in comfortable look to him, like a big sofa. He was also a footballer of the first order, having made first team at Loyola Academy as a sophomore lineman.

I learned about his football playing years later. Charley never told me about it. It just never would have occurred to him. At Loyola U. I knew him as a guy who hit the books and delivered without flash of the sort I was prone to. He wore glasses, had a sort of dumpy look to him with hair combed entirely as a convenience measure, as opposed to my own careful self-grooming with a view to female response. And he carried his many books in a leather brief case— a self-derogatory fashion statement of which he seemed happily oblivious.

He had arrived at the novitiate a year after me, having pledged my (and my brothers' before me) fraternity, Alpha Delta Gamma, a semester after I did. I had done it in in the spring of '50, he in the fall, when I was undergoing my Jesuit initiation at Milford—where we paddled ourselves, as it were, vs. being paddled by our fraternity brothers. Charley and I were both readers. His regular conversation-starter became "What are you doing for spiritual reading?" This wouldn't have been just he and I talking at first. Novices walked in threes, with a view to discouraging "particular friendship." As novices our hunger for books was limited to spiritual stuff, lives of Christ and books on meditation and the like.

As to pairing off when we were juniors, Charley wondered once why some of us seemed to belong in a circle; and others, like him and me, didn't. Some had their picnic walks lined up, others had to scramble. Some had their groups full of eager talk and laughter. From these groups others, Charley and I among them, kept their distance. We got together on the playing field, argued and debated things and enjoyed each other sporadically, as we ran into each other. But we didn't flock together in effervescence of joy at each other's company.

Charley was on to something that neither of us understood: we were in a funny situation here. We had survived the daily pressures of novitiate life, graduated, and done the life-determining thing, our vows. Now here we were, most of us in our 20s, stranded on our monastic island, brothers in a sort of pious, studious frat house. Some seemed to find the situation just fine. I never did, as much as I liked the studies.

In fact, I would consider my fellow Jesuits now and then, wondering how they seemed so at ease, when for various reasons I felt so often so ill at ease. That contradicts what I said about juniorate as happy place, but the love of study was going hand in hand with young manhood, which has its discomforts wherever encountered. In any case, we were learning how to get along without various distractions. Ours was the healthy life.

Learning how to live without drink, the young man's favorite prescription for ennui, we also had to mix our once robust prayer life with study. Some prayed at expense of study, Ed Hartman once implied. One who had set the mark for intensity of fervor as a novice as a junior stayed in chapel after breakfast faithfully until 7:55, five minutes to study time, supplementing his pre-breakfast hour and forty-five minutes of meditation, mass, and post-mass thanksgiving.

But he also got his studies done, even if you could have balanced an egg on his head while he prayed. A remarkable guy he was, one of our three or four Lithuanians who had escaped the communists. He eventually left the society as a priest and established himself as a PhD. psychological counselor, remaining a priest in good standing, I assume under an exiled Lithuanian bishop. All in all, an estimable man.

The rest of us made it to our desks by eight o'clock. And all of us, as far as I could see, made the transition from novice learning spiritual ropes to junior learning language. We did Sophocles, as I noted. I emoted with all my heart (in Greek, of course), as if the Olympian god I addressed were listening as carefully as I believed ours did in real life.

THE DIRECTOR

When the assignment came to direct the St. Stanislaus Day play, I plunged in. I picked Charley Law as my helper and got absorbed in books about dramatics. I'd never heard of Stanislavski, the great dramatics teacher, until I began plowing through whatever the juniorate library contained. I had to learn all about casting, running rehearsals, picking a play in the first place from scratch, on my own, no one to tell me what to do. Willie Ryan directed me to various sources. He was more or less moderator of it all, but from a distance.

This was typical, actually. For my practice teaching credit in the summer before my first year of "regency," I had an experienced Jesuit look in on my first two sessions—it was a repeater class in Latin—and that was it. I just taught the rest on my own. Other instances there were of a sort of benign indifference on superiors' part. It was low-key governance throughout.

Preparing to direct the play, I had the summer to get ready. We had our French classes and little else in juniorate summers, with time for reading novels and the like. I took on the "Best Plays" volumes from the 20s and later, finally choosing "George Washington Slept Here," a true chestnut that looked like fun and permitted our bending the gender of female roles. It was froth, Willie Ryan told me on the day after our performance. He meant no putdown in that, and I felt none.

Al Kezys, the Lithuanian whom I had helped to learn English and who later made his mark as a distinguished art photographer in Chicago, ran the stage crew. Here was a guy whose idea of recreation was to change the work he was doing. To the task, which he also had to learn from scratch, he brought energy and direction. Charley and I did the casting.

Rehearsals were for me an exercise in telling a lot of people what to do. One of our leads observed that I was cheap with compliments. Charley told me I'd been too hard on one guy who was slow in getting the hang of his part. This was learning how to do things with a little help from one's friends. If superiors had butted out, peers did their bit to educate each other.

The whole thing came off in our auditorium with, guess what? a full house, none of whom had anything better to do and most of whom had no say about being there in the first place but were still a great audience. For competition we had neither newspaper nor radio nor movies. Nor television, whose golden-age, live-audience years coincided in part with ours as juniors. Juniors had the Jesuit-run weekly, America, in the library, and Vital Speeches, at that time a weekly, which was not a bad way to keep up, if I had cared about it. Thumbing through America, I went always to book, play, and movie reviews in the back.

DEBATABLE

When we did get current, it was with both feet. Four of us got caught up in Sen. Joe McCarthy and his anti-communist activities as a debate topic. There was a debate about evolution—"just a theory, remember that," one of these debaters told me. I lacked strong conviction on the subject. Debates were held in front of both novices and juniors, a few each year.

When my turn came, the issue was vernacular liturgy. My partner and I defended it as the wave of the future, little knowing how right we were. Nor did I know how my opinion in the matter would change, but none of that right now, please.

It was all for the greater glory of God, in the Jesuit tradition, of course. But in debate as on the ball field, we played to win. "Is this your contribution to the greater glory of God?" a state college professor was said to have asked a Jesuit high school graduate who had routinely placed his "A.M.D.G." ("Ad majorem Dei gloriam") at the top of a poorly done paper. We weren't supposed to do poorly. Besides, it was fun to compete and more fun to win. My partner and I won our debate, as I recall. And that was fun.

All in all, not counting the stresses and strains I mentioned earlier, the juniorate played to my strong suits and my strong interests. It was bookish, with emphasis on clear and memorable expression. It was verbal. It was histrionic and oratorical and closed-circuited, meaning it was with people I knew in a familiar environment. I can still picture the library on the second floor in a corner of the building, with its shelves and windows looking out on tree-shaded, leafy grounds.

Ours was not a purely institutional setting, but part of an estate, as was not unusual for Jesuit houses of training. It's as if the Jesuits had been awaiting the dissolution of country houses in the 1920s and 30s, ready to take them off the hands of owners who couldn't afford them or didn't want them. This Milford site, however, was not donated but was bought by Xavier University in 1925.

BUDDIES

We were in the countryside, on a river, near a small suburb. From our building we could fan out in walks on country roads and wooded trails. We did so in pairs in the juniorate, bringing matches for a small fire on which to toast cheese sandwiches or fry eggs and heat coffee. There two of us would sit, propped against a tree, cooking and eating and drinking, discussing the work of the day, our world as we saw it, mocking a teacher here and there who seemed to deserve it.

We picked walk partners. As novices we had been assigned them. It was considered important to mix them up, not always pairing with a buddy. Sometimes you were to pick a non-buddy or even someone who irritated you. It was up to you to get to know the guy, try to bridge the gap—of family background, ethnicity, interests. Moved by Christian charity or community spirit, you took an interest in people you might never have talked to on the outside. I mentioned this to the novice master once and elicited a patented frown for my comment. He wasn't about to dignify that problem but sternly spoke the ideal. The idea was, just do it, without even hinting at difficulty in getting along with others. He didn't want to hear about it.

The juniorate dean, John McGrail, landed more lightly but no less tellingly. He would speak up for team sports, for instance, as opposed to swimming, running, or even handball. On a touch football or softball team, you performed as a unit. You had to communicate with each other. Running right instead of left as agreed, you screwed up the play. Going for a bad pitch and striking out, you left others in the lurch. Handball doubles qualified, but less so than six-man football or softball. Basketball too, though at Milford we had only a single backboard and were limited to three-man teams.

McGrail did not spell this out or drum home the point. He made it only once, but it stayed with me. I also remember him after a touchball game, when my team had lost and I was mad and showed it. From a group he looked at me quizzically: I responded, "Well I wanted to *win*!" I tended to overdo my response, which is why he had the look, I'm sure. When someone you respect gives you a look, you remember it. Later, when he was rector at West Baden, he spoke once publicly against shyness as doing no one any good. Suffering an attack of diffidence at the time, I paid attention.

McGrail was very important to the juniorate experience. I told him so in a letter years later. He was in his eighties at the time and was playing daily golf, I heard, almost certainly with fellow Jesuits, probably at a local daily-fee course. He died at 91 in 2002 after 74 years as a Jesuit, over 60 as a priest! He had a lifetime of being in charge of others and from all I have heard never outstayed his welcome in a half dozen or more major leadership posts. When we left Milford for West Baden, he came with us, no longer as dean but as rector. His lotus-eating days were over too.

So went the juniorate. Four Milford years were gone, four years of training completed, the normal cycle. The older ones among us did juniorate in a year or skipped it entirely, like my brother, ten years older than I. Bidding farewell on an August day in 1954 as the bus idled at the front door, I told Paul Allen, who had so encouraged writing for publication, that I would keep it up if I kept anything up in philosophy. As extracurricular, I added, when he looked briefly put off, as if I were to neglect my primary duties.

I didn't know then how sorely tempted I would be to do just that. Minutes later we were off to southern Indiana. Orange County, we were on our way.

CHAPTER 3. PHILOSOPHICAL BENT: PHILOSOPHY, 1954–57

Philosophy: Handmaiden to theology.
—as argued by Thomas Aquinas

It was on to West Baden, then—that "distillery of knowledge," as we sang in mock salute—and "the coming of the philosophic mind." As juniors we had been warned about that by a veteran priest who had just preached a short retreat, spouting poetry which he had by heart—clearly the result of a lifelong habit.

He was a rough-looking guy, a onetime coal miner, we heard, with hands to show it and a gentle, understated manner. A number of us ate the poetry up and caught up with him on the relaxed day after the retreat, he on a bench on a pleasant spring day, we sitting or standing nearby, and pumped him about the poetry. He was modest about his memorizing ability but said or implied he hadn't his old enthusiasm for it, which he attributed to the study of philosophy, that "philosophic mind." That transformation lay waiting for us.

COSMIC SHIFT

Where there had been beauty, there would be truth, or at least a way to grapple with it. Instead of John McGrail and Cicero on friendship, there were Tommy Byrne and "minor logic," a study of the basics of argument—minor as distinguished from epistemology, the frontal assault on how we know things. Tommy, a wiry little guy, personable and friendly, verbal to a fault, taught in Latin. He possessed absolute mastery of the syllogism and was dedicated to getting us through the course. He worked hard, delivered energetically, and was available for discussion in his room. An excellent technician, he plunged into the major, the minor, the inexorable conclusion—if A and B, then C, hah!—and everything in between, taking us with him as if we too could breathe under water.

I would go to his room and ask him about something I didn't get, emulating St. John Berchmans, S.J., patron of Jesuit students in training. He would respond generously, and I would leave inundated, gasping for air. It was a harbinger. In the juniorate I had moved in familiar territory. In philosophy I had to grope. A dark night of the intellect loomed before me. With the intellect in the dark, the soul would not be doing so well either.

We also had metaphysics, that bedrock of Scholastic philosophy, what Thomas Aquinas had founded or at least helped off to a roaring start 700 years earlier. This got to the essence (and existence) of things, or was billed that way. I didn't get the point of it until we spent time two years later on positivism, which I took to be its polar opposite and from which I got the point of metaphysics. Or so it seemed at the time. It was one of my two or three more or less philosophical insights in the three years. Not bad when you think about it.

And we had epistemology, cosmology, natural theology, ethics. Each attacked me in turn when I was supposed to be attacking them. The middle of any course became the point when I stopped hearing "we will get to that" about things I didn't understand and began hearing "when we covered that" about things I still didn't understand.

I missed those subjects and predicates all in a row, those Latin and Greek word endings that made all the difference, those linguistic puzzles that had answers I could figure out. I missed the drama, the characterization, the dialogue, the good, true, and beautiful in glorious, deathless classical and Shakespearean packages. Where was truth, for that matter, the supposed payoff for those who no longer had time for beauty? It was hidden deep within those damn syllogisms. It was Doctor Dryasdust time.

SO-CALLED COMMUNITY

There was more. First-year philosophers found themselves lowest on a seven-tier totem pole, beneath two classes of philosophy and four of theology, six tiers down from our recently vacated top-drawer position at Milford. This was a new kind of community life with twice as many people from all over the world.

Milford was a tight little island with little exposure to what happened beyond our 99 acres and the sleepy town and the hills and woods where we hiked and picnicked, where a trip to the local dentist was a big deal.

There were also new notions about rule observance. We had been told it separated the wannabes from the real Jesuit thing. At Milford there was an understanding about when to talk and when to talk in Latin, for instance. You knew where you stood in the matter and didn't have to think about it. At Baden there was no such understanding. You could get looked at funny if you followed rules too closely, which was annoying and something of a shock, enough to throw you off your feed.

Moreover, there were many non-Midwesterners in the mix. Take the New Yorkers. It was bad enough you couldn't always make out what they were saying, for instance. "Solt" with a long "o" meant "salt." The one asking for it might have to point. And habits might be different. The mid-town Manhattanite confessed that in his family, wine was the usual dinner drink, not beer. In ours, wine was for Christmas and Thanksgiving.

New Yorkers were bolder and more prepared to stand up for their rights. One waxed indignant at a dean's deciding what degree, Litt.B. or A.B., a philosopher should seek or an English teacher's supposed force-feeding us English majors with New Criticism, something we had no opinion about.

Marylanders were more relaxed. One of them took relaxation to new levels, giving a speech in which he praised some outlandish New York character, a social lion of sorts—no one to praise, ironically or not, in our setting. Various faculty were angered at his effrontery.

This was Tim O., a cool character, two years ahead of us, whose droll manner and easy ways put him above piddling concerns of house discipline. He was easy-going, not Eastern so much as Southern, or that peculiar Maryland Province combination of the two. He appealed to the what-the-hell part of me. Even when I was 101% for observance, I was always a sucker for the clever fellow with his own way of doing things who did not take himself too seriously.

Marylanders in general, who included Pennyslvanians, were easier to know, though one New Yorker comes to mind as a friendly, open fellow, a graduate of a Jesuit high school in New York City, Paul (Pole) Becker (Beckah). Two Marylanders in our year, Jack Britten and John Keating, were old shoes.

Keating was an athletic little guy who became part of a small-man basketball team (with one big guy) we called Liliputians. Britten was a roly-poly fellow who did something athletic once when he was very small and decided it was a bad idea. Both were English majors in our master's degree classes, which we took at the rate of one a semester as tagalong with our philosophy classes.

"You mean you like this stuff?" Keating once asked when I confessed a love for Chaucer. I could laugh that off coming from him. Britten was more dry, self-possessed, and academic in interests.

Another Marylander, Jim Sosnoski, took me to task a few years later, when I expressed dissatisfaction with Hemingway's style. We were taking summer courses at Loyola U. He couldn't abide my comment and set me straight on a number of points. I appreciated it, as much for his straightforward professional enthusiasm as for what he said.

Years later, when I was on my way out of the Jesuits, a nun friend asked what I would do for conversation. She had a point there. I have never quite matched it, though newspaper people came close.

A BIGGER COCOON

In any case, at Baden we were out of the Milford cocoon into a passable version of the wide, wide world. The local surroundings were a shock. Milford was pleasant and cozy. There was nothing cozy about West Baden Springs, a rough old spot on the highway with a gaudy, even tawdry past. The college, the former West Baden Springs Hotel, had been a resort and gambling mecca frequented by mobster Al Capone and other high rollers. It closed in 1932, done in by the Depression but also by the newly emerging Florida-vacation option.

The Jesuits came two years later with their "college," and the locals thought the brothels would have a rebirth. Disappointed, some decided it was the saltpeter—potassium nitrate, for centuries suspected of cooling sexual ardor—slipped into our soup that explained our continence. On this point, Cecil Adams of "Straight Dope" fame at the Chicago Reader, debunking the notion, has wisdom to offer: "All in all, there's still no substitute for the cold shower." That and meditation, the Jesuits would say.

The building itself was grand and cold. Lee Wiley Sinclair had built it in 1901, installing a huge dome supported by the walls, 100 feet high at its apex (world's highest until the Houston Astrodome in 1965, with its 208 feet), over a gorgeous terrazzo-tiled "atrium" floor, a sort of promenade and indoor plaza in the round.

The supporting walls had guest rooms that faced the atrium and others that faced outdoors, making for five floors of circular corridors. The inner rooms were for library and utility space. The dome was unsupported by pillars, of course. But Brother Fred Snyder, the aged, sweet little guy who as "porter" greeted tourists, when asked by one of them how the dome was supported, reportedly answered, "By free will offerings." Not a bad answer from the guileless Brother Freddy.

ACTUALLY LEARNING SOMETHING

As for what went on under the dome, even in view of my earlier rant, we did learn something, notwithstanding various degrees of befuddlement produced by Tommy Byrne (not a complete loss either) and others. We were at least exposed to the philosophical mind, some of which rubbed off on us. In fact, some bright lights shone during this time. Joe Wulftange taught cosmology, scholastic philosophy's shot at explaining the material world. Joe came into class each day with sheets neatly typed on a very good Courier 12 electric typewriter and run off on the mimeograph. They were the latest pages of a philosophy of science he was developing at the time, in the fall of 1954.

Two years earlier, he had delivered a paper, "Hylomorphism and

Contemporary Physics," to a Jesuit Philosophical Association meeting, hylomorphism being Aristotle's analysis of things according to matter ("hylo") and form ("morph"). He was trying to bridge a gap, I gather.

Joe held the received cosmology in genial contempt, ignoring a long-used textbook in Latin, *Cosmologia*, by a Jesuit named Hoenen (rhymes with Noonan). We each were given our Hoenen, as if to satisfy a requirement, but if any of us read or consulted it, he stayed quiet about it. If Murel "Doc" Vogel, the dean, ever asked about it, or had to satisfy others above him who asked, Wulftange could say his students had their Hoenen, I guess. But he found no use for it in our course.

It was from Wulftange that I got one of my rare insights, in this case the concept of mathematical formula as language, expressing what could not otherwise be expressed. From him I got at least a feel for the concept of formula (or theory) as workable (conditionally verified) or not. He made me a smidgen more sophisticated about scientific method. It was the sort of introduction that enables one at least to catch on to a conversation. In this it was liberalizing and clearly related to the world of learning. Much of what we received was not.

I was not alone in profiting from him. Art McGovern, a Jesuit contemporary of mine with long tenure at the University of Detroit, credited him in later years with imparting an open-mindedness towards "adversaries."

Naming lifetime influences, he cited Wulftange as "the most influential teacher [he] had as a Jesuit seminarian," insisting as he did, "counter to the prevailing method of 'refuting adversaries,'" that his students were not to criticize adversaries until they understood them. When McGovern in his European studies in philosophy approached

Marxism, therefore, he did so "as objectively as possible, following Wulftange's advice."

Doc Vogel, the dean, taught "natural theology," about God as known by reason alone. He was a cheery fellow, but suspicious. Or so I found him when, naively, I went to him as dean with what I thought was a great idea: How about us philosophers putting on a play? I was only a few months into philosophy, which I hated, and was looking to relive juniorate glory or at least fun. Unfortunately, unbeknownst to me, someone had just come to him with the same idea, and he smelled a rat. He berated me for applying pressure to him. I left with tail between legs.

Indeed, Baden was no humanist's delight. Approaching philosophy as if it might be a continuance of the liberal education we had begun at Milford, I was sorely disappointed. I was no more to find it there than a law student would find it in law school. This was professional training, imparting discipline and data. Doc Vogel was perfectly within his portfolio not to want us play-acting. Lotus-eaters needed not apply at West Baden.

For each there was an out, however, namely our master's degree courses. We needed the master's degree to teach high school or as a start to seeking a Ph.D. Mine was in English literature. Our teacher was Fred Manion, a pudgy little guy with neatly combed receding black hair and a warm smile—the soul of conviviality. He'd been to Oxford—among us was a sprinkling of Oxonians—and in any case was careful, methodical, and alert. He was quite good at what he was doing.

I found myself relying on the English course, one a semester, as respite from logic and metaphysics and epistemology, in due time succeeded by natural theology, ethics, philosophical psychology, and I forget what else. Cosmology, as I've said, was memorable, what with Joe Wulftange arriving each day with a new set of notes, fresh off his teeming brain. It could be that his subject was ripe for dismissal in its previous state, when others were not. Or not yet. Years later, the scholastic philosophy preference was abandoned.

GROWING UP HIGHER

Meanwhile, there was the matter of managing one's personal growth, to use a going phrase. The Milford-bred emphasis on rule-keeping was not easily dismissed. For instance, my brother Jerry, ten years older than I, he who had met me at the novitiate door four years earlier, was on the other side of the house, in theology. He had left Milford a week or so after I'd arrived and gone to Baden for philosophy, skipping juniorate. That put him two years up on the youngsters he had entered with—who had admired him greatly, I heard often from them. He'd done philosophy in two years, as he had skipped juniorate, having a Jesuit degree, cutting a year more off the usual requirement, and then done teaching in two, cutting off another. Now, four years up on his novice classmates, he was back for the four of theology which permitted no cutting.

He used to visit me now and then after night examen, during the time of "sacred silence," when we were expected to compose ourselves for the morning's meditation. I would hear him coming down the hall and await his knock on my door. (We had private rooms after four years of Milford dormitories.) It was against the rules, and that bothered me, but I was glad to see him. I knew that if it weren't for him, I might not even be there. His entry into the Jesuits had given me the idea of doing so. I also knew he would not buy my thinking about rule observance and there'd be uncomfortable tension as a result. So I put up with the conflict. I found it uncomfortable but swallowed it nonetheless. But as I saw it, I was backtracking.

At other times I did not give way, as when I gave to the minister of the house the fine alarm clock sent by two aunts for Christmas—and telling them I did so. It would never have come to me at Milford, nor would they have sent it, but they understood (correctly) that things were different at Baden. I wrote and explained that we weren't allowed to keep gifts, which we weren't, without permission. Besides, we were to pursue evangelical poverty by getting along with less. They knew a lot of Jesuits who took gifts, however, and must have chalked up my refusal to youthful enthusiasm, naivete, or just plain ignorance. But they never commented.

But consider that I was not quite 24 when I refused the clock. Most 24-year-olds were working for a living. Many were married with children. But I was sifting through whether to keep an alarm clock and was suffering pangs of conscience for various rules violations such as talking to my brother when he'd come by to visit me after hours.

The anomaly was captured by a philosopher a year or so older than I, a Detroiter with a deceptively abstracted manner. Learning that a dishwasher in the kitchen, a local fellow about 20 years old, had three kids, he marveled whimsically that he himself had not yet acquired "an adequate concept of being," which was one of the philosophical conundrums that engaged us in those days.

Wrestling with minor considerations in a closed-circuit atmosphere was hardly the stuff of either heroism or maturity—though indeed there's no perfect way to acquire direction for one's life. We had been cocooned at Milford. The further cocooning at West Baden was another matter, partly because we were older.

As for our continuing education, it was in its way businesslike. We were doing some hard thinking, if nothing else. At Milford we had our eyes opened to the glory that was Greece and the grandeur that was Rome. At Baden we had them opened to the power of cold, clear reason.

SOCIAL ETHICS

We had daily newspapers too. The Chicago Tribune and Louisville Courier-Journal appeared regularly in our rec room. So if I wanted to go beyond book and movie reviews in America Magazine, I could do so. We were a potentially influential group, which is why one group sought our membership in a mailing. This was the newly established Intercollegiate Society of Individualists (ISI)—free-marketers who wanted to convert us Jesuits to the cause.

At least two popes had got there first, however, Leo XIII and Pius XI, in their encyclicals which rejected "rugged individualism." As a papist of the first water, I couldn't buy what ISI (still existing, newly named with same initials) was selling. I responded to their pitch, quoting the popes, and they took me off their list. This was too bad. I could have used some free-market thinking in the years ahead. Indeed, I am more inclined to think these days that the popes were victims of bad advice, as by German Jesuits working for Pius XI who were unduly influenced by German political theory.

In any case, thus died a free-market tinge to my socio-political mentality. A few years later, I fumed at William F. Buckley's dismissal of John XXIII's "Mater et Magistra"—"Mater si, magistra no"—in which Catholic "social doctrine" (actually social "advice" or exhortation) was reiterated and expanded. How dare he? He had no heart. Worse, he had no obedience to go with his Catholicism.

His dissent represented something of an advance in the independence of lay people. but I was part of no such advance. As a loyalist and in my way a company man, I rejected conservatism anew and bought the liberal (better "neo-liberal), near-statist option, though involving salubrious hostility to Marxism, of course, as corrective. In any case, to endorse a position was to act on it. A religious-motivated conversion to social liberalism was a call to action, if I may use a phrase that became a Catholic (neo-)liberal rallying cry, then a conference, then a Chicago-based national organization of many decades standing, even to this day.

I didn't buy statism whole, in large part thanks to Paul Kennedy, whose social ethics course was based on scholastic philosophers. He was a hard-headed guy who didn't stand on ceremony, rough-hewn and impatient. His friend Reggie Lefevour, who taught psychology, was a sweet-tempered guy impossible to dislike but tempting as a target. So was Kennedy for his mannerisms, but we couldn't take his lectures lightly.

Kennedy used a good deal of Latin terminology in class, where theoretically Latin, if I may garble the message, was to be the *lingua franca*. His friend Lefevour and others let it go with a phrase now and then, however. Not so with the oral exams at year end, which were in Latin. Lefevour belabored points with simple, even cute examples: if the dog had a mind, he could not *not* talk, double negative to the forefront.

It was the sort of thing a fairly clever high school teacher could toss out and make stick, or in his case a fairly clever psychology teacher in a Jesuit philosophate in the '50s. What he said might come in handy some day. No elaborate argument there, pretty much canned, but illustrative and in its way effective.

Kennedy, on the other hand, was to be taken seriously no matter whom we would be teaching later on. He delivered his Latin with a pronunciation all his own, his a's flat as pancakes, in a loud clear voice mildly inhibited by incipient phlegm. Probably in his late 50s, he was vigorous but walked as if he'd injured his knees on a playing field, though we never heard of him playing anything. He never played golf on our nine-hole course preserved from the old hotel days.

In fact, I can't recall seeing him ever outside the building doing anything. But he had a mind to remember and would present his arguments and overall treatment of Aquinas and followers on property, justice, and the like coherently. He provided a nice hard-headed corrective to papal rhetoric, which was homiletic to an extreme and the product to large extent of the German Jesuit Oswald von Nell-Breuning, himself a product of German leaning toward statism. (For what it's worth, Nell-Breuning felt used in the process, not by the pope but by the Jesuit general, Father Wlodimir Lechowski, who approved the final product with an eye to Italian and Vatican politics, Nell-Breuning said much later.)

In any case, it should be said, with all my retrospective complaining, that we were doing more than playing brain golf, though it felt sometimes as if we were doing nothing else. Brain aerobics is a better term. We were tackling ideas, if somewhat narrowly as to method. No class called for reading books, for instance! There was no reference to current commentary, not much open-ended inquiry, at least in the first two of our three years, when we pursued the core scholastic philosophy curriculum. We acquired no familiarity with journals. Discussion was limited.

While a spirit of criticism was surely part of the mix, it was with a view to refuting "adversarii." Indeed, every thesis was introduced with a "state of the question," definitions, and enumeration of "adversarii," the other guys. As I say above in the matter of positivism vs. scholastic metaphysics, I learned more about the latter from learning more about the former. If we had heard and considered adversaries' ideas first, with a nod to how they hindered the pursuit of wisdom, we might have been more interested in the solutions we were expected to endorse.

The education was less liberal than professional. We worked towards a church-authorized "licentiate," which would license us, as it were, for delivery of approved teaching. Each year ended with an oral exam in Latin, a half hour for first and second years, an hour for third. This last was the "de universa,"—"day you" was the going designation—"about everything," on the whole of philosophy as we knew it.

Flunk one of these, and you were in the "short course," where you got less detail and profundity. I didn't flunk, partly because Latin had no mysteries for me. But at the end of theology, I did badly enough not to be approved for so-called solemn vows, to be taken two or three years after completing the training. I did well enough to get the S.T.L., or theology licentiate, however, as a consolation prize. More later about that.

LASTING EFFECTS

The training was professional, but it couldn't help being more than that. We had our noses rubbed in philosophy, for two years nothing but the scholastic variety. But in the third we branched out. Bob Harvanek was back from a year in Germany, where he had an awakening of sorts. With him and Doc Vogel and others, we looked at "adversarii" such as Kant and the American pragmatist Charles Sanders Peirce. (For Peirce say "purse." More later about that.)

Immanuel Kant did me in. I had a spacious room on the top, fifth, floor with double exposure, having had an early pick because I was a third-year man. In that lovely room I pretty near broke my head on the Critique of Pure Reason. I decided later that Kant was a bad writer, like most of his ilk.

However, the three years of exposure to serious thinking fostered an interest in such matters. At least it gave a sort of gentleman's awareness of issues. In years to come I would know or at least strongly suspect that there's more to things than meet the eye. I was developing a certain caution in the face of a conundrum, which has its uses. That old philosophical mind again.

Yes, there was approved and non-approved thinking. But we were big on argument and took learning and criticism seriously. We learned to find all things discussable and nothing disgusting, which has its drawbacks, to be sure. In the gardens of our mind, next to the orthodoxy which we felt bound to defend reasonably, grew our humanistic liberalism.

In my post-Jesuit life, I now and again ran into friendly or not friendly accusations of being "just like a Jesuit" or simply "a Jesuit" (once a Jesuit, always a Jesuit was the message), when I would press for data to back something up. At a newspaper guild meeting, I was accused of being a Jesuit when I implied that I'd respect another union's work stoppage depending on its case. I was supposed to embrace union solidarity no matter what. On another occasion, at an Oak Park gathering, I questioned a social cause, asking what the data were, and was again accused of being a Jesuit, this time by a fellow ex-Jesuit.

Being a newsman encouraged that. As a reporter, I heard out the presumed ideological enemy—conservative Lutheran-Missouri Synod leaders, for example. It was part of my job. So was the discipline of not letting on where I stood on an issue, for which I was once congratulated by an Oak Park activist surprised at my ability to pull this off. The Daily News editor, Roy Fisher, once passed on a similar compliment from a fellow Methodist who was reacting to a column I did about an early-'70s Methodist dustup. I was also nailed at times for unfairness, not always inaccurately, but I never doubted the goal.

The lesson from both Jesuit training and newspaper-reporter learning on the job was that you need evidence, not to mention clarity and consistency. When a Jesuit friend accused me of "playing the logic game" in an argument about the resurrection of Jesus, about which more later, he was going at a whole mindset of mine. I was married with kids, and he was teaching theology from an endowed chair at Loyola, for one thing which made me more likely to play the logic game. Being married with kids does that to a fellow. For another, as a reporter I had to be more hard-headed about things.

THE THIRD YEAR

In any case, West Baden contributed to intellectual development. Nor did all the knowledge we gained make a bloody entrance. Joe Wulftange awakened interest, as I have said. So did Bob Harvanek, a learned man who never stopped learning. He taught us history of philosophy in our first year and more recent, non-scholastic philosophy in our third.

But he was not the same Bob Harvanek the second time. He'd spent a year in Germany, immersed in study and discussion and intellectual ferment and from it had emerged a sort of kinder, gentler Harvanek, to adapt a well-worn phrase. The change came from some sort of insight he had gained into "community," I heard, as if he'd experienced a softening influence after years of discipline.

Whatever happened, he was full of interesting stuff, almost none of which I recall, but that's beside the point. In this case, we had a mind at work before our very eyes, ideal for the third year of our two-one program, as it was called—two years of meeting a requirement, one of expanding horizons.

In this year we weren't grubbing for basics, going from state of the question, definitions, "adversarii" to be refuted, to theses proven by adept use of major, minor, and conclusion. This was stuff that contributed probably more than anything else to the Jesuit mindset that I said was noticed by others in later years. To have a mind like a trap was the goal: bang, bang, click, click. I do not reject it. It's a way to avoid being fooled. There's so much nonsense in the world, it's good to guard against it with a little logic.

In this third year, on the contrary, we were allowed to get adventurous, spending time with adversaries. Not that I was up to it, by the way. Kant I have mentioned. I tried reading Hegel to no avail. Turgid stuff. Impatient, I tried speed-reading Hegel, with no better results, needless to say. It was nice to have more time to ourselves, but I felt out of my depth.

Doc Vogel seemed not wholly comfortable with this looser approach. Finding us unresponsive on one occasion, having failed to do the reading, he complained. "You don't want to be spoon-fed, but then you don't perform." This free-wheeling third year was something of an experiment, which he didn't think was working out.

He wasn't the only one suffering from discontent. An undercurrent ran through student ranks. Why wouldn't there be? There we were, still largely regimented and either bored or befuddled much of the time, depending on the quantity of one's gray matter, without nights on the town or fun, even innocent, with the opposite sex, without family responsibilities, presumably absorbed in our studies, in our prayer such as it was, and in ourselves, as is common for people our age. It was a climate for trouble, at least within the bodies and souls of each individually.

MAKING DO

We always had sports or listening to classical music or hiking-and-picnicking or b.s.'ing each other. This could be rewarding, as I have implied. We enjoyed each other, and rec-room banter produced a gem now and then.

For instance, we read in the Chicago Trib one day of a priest named in a "balm suit" in which a cuckolded husband sought compensation for his pain. "What's balm?" someone asked. "Ecclesiastical sperm," said another, and there you have celibate-bachelor humor, rough-cut. Indeed, for holy abstainers we got fairly direct at times with our comments. Verbal to a fault, you know.

We had our hikes and picnics, as I said. There was a cabin up in the hills for us philosophers, where we could heat cheese sandwiches over a fire. (Fun, eh?) Theologians had their own cabin. We were to keep clear of each other except on "fusion" days, as novices and juniors kept clear of each other at Milford. I drank my first coffee in such a cabin, black and tasty. And I began drinking it regularly thereafter, to stay awake in class. In Tommy Byrne's logic class in first year, for instance. He commented once on our dozing off, that he had seen us running around on the ball field an hour before but had no life in us come class time. Coffee became the solution.

At meals here as at Milford, none but the rector had a set place, except that faculty sat at his table and the one next to it, facing the pulpit. "Divisions" were observed: theologians, philosophers, brothers all at separate tables. Seated, we heard reading by a scholastic from the book of the week or month—a biography of Cardinal Gibbons of Baltimore or Franklin D. Roosevelt or a history of the Jesuits or—this I remember well—*With God in Russia*, by Walter Ciszek, a Jesuit who infiltrated the Soviet Union to minister to the dwindling faithful. He told his story to Dan Flaherty, a Chicago Jesuit who entered two or three years before me and was for a time an editor at America Magazine. It was a gripping account.

We also had books about Red China, exposes quietly resented by one left-leaning classmate as misrepresenting the communist experiment and fanning anti-communism among us. A few years later at St. Ignatius High, Chicago, on the other hand, a book about FDR sent a veteran teacher to the kitchen for his night meal, so incensed was he by its favorable treatment of That Man in the White House. Indeed, this man had his own stationery which gave the school's address as 1076 W. 12th Street, rather than Roosevelt Road (after Teddy, not Franklin, by the way), its current name. He did not want to have to announce to anyone that his street bore that deeply resented name.

FUN

At Baden we had wine on feast days. There were various classes of these. For first-class feasts such as Christmas and Easter and the feast of St. Ignatius, the kitchen went all out. Two wines were served, dry with the meal, sweet with dessert. Second-class feasts— lesser saints' days—merited only dry. It was at the West Baden table that I learned the sweet-dry difference, using the rule of thumb, 18% alcohol label for sweet, 12% for dry. It was Novitiate wine, from Los Gatos, California, where California Province novices worked the vineyards.

To beer, which was rarely served at table, I needed no introduction. That and bourbon and gin were staples of any party our family ever had, with a taste of wine for Christmas and after-dinner liqueurs, including creme de menthe and creme de cocoa (with a small layer of cream on top, laid on by my father) and benedictine and brandy— "b-and-b." Neither did I need introduction to hard liquor, except to drink it, which I hadn't done as an 18-year-old.

I still learned something here and there, as about scotch from a Cincinnatian, later posted to South America, who told me, overstating the case, that there were no bad versions of scotch, in contrast with bourbon or blends. In any case, scotch had a "burnt" taste, as did Irish, he said. I was being liberally educated in these matters, and in genteel fashion.

This fellow was two or three years my senior and had three or four years of college before entering. So I took his word for it. Besides, he became a regional superior for U.S. Jesuits in Peru and deserves respect for that, if not for his rank among connoisseurs. Like many Cincinnatians he was a baseballer who merely played at other sports. He became for me a good sounding board in these years of training.

He also provided a political conservatism for me to absorb and resist, on one occasion indignantly observing that a driver's license application referred to driving as a privilege revocable by the state. "A privilege," he said, taking this as a symbol of the road to serfdom we were all traveling. On another occasion he noted that U.S. cities had "the best-dressed poor" people, this time seeking to debunk some of my more fervent denunciations of the status quo.

He wasn't the only one who spotted me as a bomb-thrower in need of a cold conservative shower. A Chicago South Sider once angrily threw "nigger" in my face in the rec room in front of others. This was in theology, after my teaching, or regency, when I'd become notorious and annoying to some for my promotion of interracialism.

Whatever I said by way of soft answer on this occasion—I still had that Christian norm in my mind, not to mention the need for brothers to live together in peace—I turned away his wrath, and thereafter found him a genial friend.

I was also an admirer of Martin Luther King, and soft answers were my preferred rebuttal. In any case, at least during philosophy, I was so committed to non-violence, if only because it violated "tactus," that I once did a culpa before the entire community for "flagrant violation" of it, after blowing my lid on the basketball court and courting a fight—which I walked away from, by the way. Can you imagine what sort of second-guessing of oneself goes into such a sequence? Examined life indeed.

In due time, the South Sider and others slid back from their resistance to change, and it's quite likely that if the road analogy be useful, he and I met each other years later going in opposite directions, he the Jesuit-for-life, I the husband and father who got conservative, or as I would put it, reasonable.

This was thirty years before I read Frederick Hayek, who confirmed my growing conviction that much if not most social change imposed by government made matters worse, not better. This made for a major, major change in my thinking, generated by many years of fretting about social justice and doing my bit, as in various organizing, demonstrating and marching.

GAMES

Meanwhile, we lived relatively high on the hog at Baden, while limited as to where we went and what we did for recreation. I sneaked into town once in theology a few years later to see "Gone With the Wind"—with guilt, fear, and trembling, though it was after

I'd been a teacher, when I'd been a responsible producer. We had our hikes and picnics, and sports. Too much of all that, according to a German friend who joined us later in theology, who expressed amazement at how much time we Americans put in on recreation.

He also once mocked my "heroic brother," a 30-mission veteran as a Flying Fortress tail gunner before being shot down and made a prisoner. Carl my German friend had been on the receiving end of American bombs and gave in this time to otherwise suppressed or at least unexpressed resentment. So. I had joined the Jesuits and without seeing the world got an education in what parts of it were thinking. Ditto the Brazilians and Venezuelans and the rest who resented the grotesque of the Mexican bandit in the Bogart film "High Sierra," which I welcomed as entetainment. West Baden was a gathering place of foreigners, whom we of course learned to call international students.

As for Carl, there was something of the superior-European view in his criticism of our recreational excesses. We did have a daily dose of it if we wished, the assumption being that we needed it in view of our long hours of study and as preventative to impure thoughts or going off our rockers. It was Reggie Lefevour, I believe, who spoke of rainy days when we couldn't get out as times of increased venial sinning among us. It was a good half-joke.

Handball was a major outlet, played usually in doubles on our outdoor one-wall courts. This was not patty-cake. You could get pushed around. Ed Skrzypczak (say "Skripjack") from Detroit almost lost an eye as he looked back at the wrong time and caught a shot from another player. He didn't lose it. If he had, Japan would have had a one-eyed Jesuit missionary a few years later, and the collection *Japan's Modern Century* (Sophia University Press, 1968) would have had a one-eyed editor.

Another incipient world-class scholar, who later got an Oxford doctorate in classics while also rowing for Oxford, had arrived at Milford a raw stripling at 17. But he filled out and beefed up, in the process acquiring a take-no-prisoners attitude on the handball court. He it is also who wrote a paper on the philosopher Charles Sanders Peirce (say "purse," remember), calling it "Who Steals My Peirce Steals Trash," which got his teacher Bob Harvanek's cork to the Nth degree. Harvanek, Father Harvanek to us scholastics, came to his room to tell him what he thought of such sophomoric precocity, knocked, heard "Come in," and was greeted with "Hi, Harv." Brash fellow.

This fellow had research-paper-writing and scholarship-by-absorption down cold. He was a machine for classwork. At Oxford he compiled a grammar for an obscure ancient language (not obscure to him). It had to be something original; Oxford doctorates did not come cheap. He was also, as I say, a prodigious handballer, who could bounce you off the court with a quick move at the ball, making of it a contact sport akin to ice hockey.

Contact happened, as "tactus" went by the boards in the playing field. I've mentioned covering third in a softball game and being sent flying with a slide, turning over in the air and landing (safely) on my back. I slid hard and low myself into a beefy catcher, my head bumping the ground behind me.

Oh, the athletic memories: a line drive hit as a novice, a double-play pivot as a junior, an over-shoulder football catch in philosophy. Don't say sports don't matter: they remain in the consciousness for years. It was *mens sana in corpore sano* for us. And it was better to daydream about baseball than girls.

BROTHERS

Another handballer of note was my cousin, Dave Bowman, once a lineman for Loyola Academy, for whom he played in one game with a broken arm, he told me. He joined the West Baden theology faculty with his newly acquired doctorate from Gregorian University in 1954, a banner Bowman year in that my brother and I arrived there also, my brother for theology. There were other brother combinations in those days, but no two-brothers-plus-cousin combination, as far as I know. And philosopher-theologian-faculty member at that.

Dave combined taking his vocation very seriously with brash and iconoclastic moments. When my English teacher Fred Manion, his contemporary, innocently recommended Mackinlay Kantor's *Andersonville*, a Civil War novel that got graphic about homosexuality in the prison camp, the rector objected. Word got out, and Dave hollered at Fred across the atrium in mock accusation, "Hey, Manion, what are you doing handing out dirty books?" Fred, not embarrassed, rolled with punches, his face breaking into full smile mode at the gibe.

Dave got himself out of Baden after a few years and went ecumenical in a big way, teaching at the U. of Iowa for a while, then working at the National Council of Churches and spending a good deal of time in Northern Ireland, where one of his nieces, over there to help him, found a husband. This was a daughter of Dave's youngest sister (of three), Margaret Hopkins, the widow for many years of an FBI agent from a Cleveland family which had given two other brothers, Joe and Jack, to the Jesuits. So it was in those days of church vocations in the 40s and 50s. Major parts of and sometimes whole families went into religion.

Among brother combinations in the Jesuits, I found the Kempers especially fascinating. They were Aloysius, Joe, and Frank.

Aloysius C. Kemper, on whom "Ack-ack" was bestowed in honor of his initials and presumably his verbal delivery, came across to the young Jesuit as the complete ascetic. When he came to Milford to give a triduum, it was as if another world had sent its emissary. He appeared sober and serious, with nothing of the humorous about him but nothing quite irritating either.

Frank Kemper was another story. He had been a missionary and looked a rumpled, old-shoe kind of guy, more proof of Jesuit catholicity. We had all kinds, and so did the Kemper family, which was of Toledo, by the way, whence came Bernie Wernert the novice master. Joe Kemper I knew from juniorate days, when he'd been our spiritual father, giving us on many an evening "points for meditation" and being on hand to hear our problems if we wanted to tell him. A wise counsellor, he was.

Another pair stood out from novitiate days, the Hogans—Bill and Tom—a pair of genial Chicagoans who sang. Bill had a tenor voice to wake the angels, or at least distract them from their appointed tasks. He and his voice were part of a magic novitiate moment. After a fairly ascetical Advent in our first year, when there was no mail from home or anywhere else, we had a Christmas Eve that was muted by popular standards, though anticipation ran high. In this case it was big kids, expecting great things. There would be a mass at midnight after a half hour of meditation; we knew that much. We went to bed earlier than our usual nine o'clock.

At eleven, sound asleep in our cubicles, we were awakened by Bill Hogan with his "O Holy Night" tenor solo as part of the juniors' choir. For the exceedingly religious late adolescent, it made for quite an imitation of dying and going to heaven. For five or ten minutes, he and they sang in the halls, we listened in our beds. Then the bell clanged, and we were up and at 'em for meditation and mass.

There was nothing like this in philosophy, which came to a halt at the close of our seventh year as Jesuits. Before us, after all that praying and studying, lay teaching. It came not a moment too soon.

FRIENDS

Meanwhile, in the course of philosophy I had unburdened myself in letters to Sister Monica, my 6th-grade teacher, who was in Chicago on assignment, probably at a parish school. She was of the Sisters of Mercy, good-looking, full of personality, smart. When I had shown up for class after missing the first few days, probably with a "bilious" stomach, she had greeted me with a smile: "Something new has been added," she said, using a phrase from a cigarette ad. Monica (Burke, we discovered, which says something about her easy openness with us boys) would stand out in front of the school on Washington Boulevard, the wind blowing her habit from which, glory be! slipped wisps of hair.

We thought nuns were bald under the black veil, and the others were, for all we knew. Not Monica, who would catch the strands and tuck them back with an easy smile. In class she put up with nothing but understood everything. Her piety was straightforward and never exaggerated. She manifested no quirks, was open and encouraging. "You're sure of yourself," she told me once when I stuck to my guns on a disputed point of learning. It was the first time I'd heard of that as a good thing.

In her lap I dumped my woes, complaining about my studies. She countered wisely with a description of nuns' life in the 40s and 50s: hitting the classroom without a degree, which they got in the summers at a Catholic college. It took many hot summers in long black habits, then returning to clean house for each other. Her story sobered me a bit, telling me I did not have it so bad, which I did not. From her I got a sort of chins-up. Many years later I visited her in retirement at St. Xavier's University on the South Side, bringing one of our kids. I didn't go to see her often enough.

CHAPTER 4. BENDING TWIGS: TEACHING, 1957–1960

'Tis education forms the common mind,
Just as the twig is bent, the tree's inclined.
                              —Alexander Pope

After philosophy came teaching, but first I had some business to handle, about going overseas to be a missionary. Some years earlier, I had written the provincial announcing my availability. Theoretically all of us were available, but they wanted volunteers. If we wanted to be Francis Xaviers, it had to be our idea.

For motivation we had Xavier's example and the whole-burnt sacrificial offering recommended for followers of the kingdom. "God HATES rapine on the holocaust," thundered a fellow junior in a rousing dinner-time sermon. No stealing from the holocaust for me. "Take, Lord, and receive," I said at vow time, and I meant every word.

But my letter to the provincial had been the end of it as far as I knew. India might call others—traditionally after juniorate, and there I was, after philosophy—but it didn't call me, and I forgot about it. Five years later, the provincial reminded me about it. Just as I was starting my summer's practice teaching at Ignatius, he called. A last-minute opening had turned up on the Nepal Express.

This was a one-way trip at the time, ticket not refundable. You went and returned God knew when and certainly not soon. India had been the choice until a year or so previously. By 1957, it was closed off to new missionaries for reasons of postcolonial politics. Instead, there was the Hidden Kingdom of Nepal, recently opened to the world by an India-based Chicago Jesuit, Marshall Moran, who talked the king of Nepal into letting us in. Three had gone a year earlier, from West Baden.

Was I interested? It was a shocking request. God hates rapine. Take and receive. And me digging in for three years at Ignatius, the mother ship in the heart of Chicago, where Father Damen had cast anchor 100 years earlier at Holy Family Church next door. Teaching English, where my treasure lay and my heart also. Surprised, caught napping.

But I was 25, and the world beckoned. I liked the idea. I would go! Take a few days, said the provincial. Tell your parents, meaning extend them the courtesy of being the first to know. Get back to me.

I drove out to Oak Park that night, and yes, it was a dark and rainy one, taking the newly opened Eisenhower Expressway. In our Lombard Avenue living room, I gave them the news, unwisely not anticipating their shocked response or more accurately, my response to theirs. The father, trying to talk himself into the idea, quoted what he had heard at a Barrington retreat: We are born to die, which was not what I had in mind at all. The mother looked stricken. Dear Mother.

In that house at 17, I had easily brushed off my father's irritation at my being told to wait a year before applying to the Jesuits. I had been firm about it. I would wait the year, I had told him, such was my confidence as a young man deciding for himself in a supportive family environment. Eight years later it was another story

I drove back to Ignatius stunned, and next day I was telling the provincial I wanted a few more days. My father was clearly relieved. In the end I didn't go, of course—a good thing for one wife, six kids, and what I came to call my delayed vocation to married life. Not that I anticipated any of that. Rather, an unforeseen wave of emotion had done me in.

My mother and father worried that I had turned down Nepal for their sakes. I denied it when my Jesuit brother passed on their concerns, dissembling. It was like my not telling the wise guy that my father had refused to sign permission for me to play football as a high school freshman. He was razzing me for not playing, but I wouldn't say why. It was none of his business, of course, and in this case it was none of theirs. It was my decision, and I wasn't going to saddle them with it. Anyhow, sadder but wiser about myself, I began my teaching.

The parents still wondered about me. A few years later, as I showed signs of discontent while not yet ordained, my father caught himself in the middle of family banter, "Once a Jesuit, always a . . . " then stopping, to say ". . . nice guy." Chances are they had picked up this sense of my uncertainty from my brother. I kept my counsel in these matters, which is not advised: you're supposed to talk things out. I did so with Jesuit friends but not with family.

This led to some bafflement on my father's part. On one occasion he spoke in roundabout fashion, just he and I in conversation, about the difficulty he had understanding me which he shared with my brother and which he had experienced with his (also older) brother. I didn't pursue it. But at this point, when my father's memory is a recurring source of consolation to me, it doesn't matter, along with a lot of other things that don't matter.

Meanwhile, as to my Jesuit life, I hung in, employing enthusiasm for the work and a certain devil-may-careness as a shield. If my father and brother could not understand me, let them join the club, I figured. I had done so. It wasn't a very happy club, but there was at least strength in numbers.

TO THE BARRICADES

As for the state of my soul in 1957, after seven years I continued to pray, trying my best to slap on over my discontent a nice coating of religious devotion. And I mostly did my duty, not turning left onto Roosevelt Road, my metaphor for jumping ship, as I descended the ancient wooden staircase at Ignatius, but right toward the classroom where 2-D English was waiting.

They were a challenge, to be sure, but also fun on wheels, once literally so when I found several pushing a radiator around the room on a dolly, one of them riding it. You may ask what the radiator and dolly were doing in the classroom, but Ignatius was an old building and maintenance was ongoing, and you found things like stray, unattached radiators.

The scene struck me so funny that my shouted desist order had a certain I-don't-give-a-damn quality that got instant response. 2-D's 41 students—yes, in one room—were red-blooded American sophomore boys, smart enough to be a challenge to me without quite mastering the subject at hand. I found it a strain but also a saving grace in that they (and their counterparts in other classes) provided for me an object for attention besides myself.

Bob Harvanek had the right idea. At this point or later, when he was director of studies for the province, he heard me out as to my supposed troubles and said he did not expect me to walk away from them because I was "not that kind of man." He was a guy who could get away with calling you to be a certain kind of man, which is what it came down to, Jesuit or not.

THE NEIGHBORHOOD

I was one of a bumper-crop dozen or so scholastics at Ignatius. We had our separate "rec room," or lounge, overlooking Roosevelt Road, where we gathered after the night meal. I don't recall having television. If we did, the reception wasn't very good. The fathers and brothers, only two or three of the latter, had their rec room one floor higher in the two-storey-high community library, with shelves on a balcony reached by a rickety staircase.

Our rec room faced the projects—ABLA Homes, which stretched a half-mile west and south to the tracks, beyond which lay the Pilsen neighborhood, once Bohemian, already becoming Mexican. Kitty-corner, stretching south and east, was what black residents called Jewtown—old, dingy, dilapidated but not public, housing. Jewtown was a Dickensian blot, black like the projects but considered tougher. Russian Jews – "the worst kind," wrote a Jesuit brother in an early history of Holy Family parish – had settled there at the turn of century.

Barney Rasofsky grew up there. His father cuffed him when he came home cuffed by toughs in the street: no son of Rasofsky was going to be a streetfighter. But Barney, turned Barney Ross, became world champion. He held three titles at once, then joined the Marines, got shot up in the South Pacific, came back with a heroin habit after taking morphine for the pain, kicked the habit, becoming yet another kind of hero. The sabbath was honored in the Rasofsky household, which shut down every Friday at sundown.

It was not honored in the convenience store on Roosevelt kitty-corner from Ignatius, where its students would wander in during lunch hour—unwisely, said Father Whitehead, a veteran Latin teacher, in a faculty meeting, because the place was full of "hopheads."

The customers were black. So was the young woman with whom the white proprietor pulled away from the curb in his convertible one spring day, waved off by neighborhood men. This was 1958, remember: the revolution had not started. The good-looker would have been congratulated on her good fortune, as would the proprietor. You could see it all from our fourth floor.

MIXING WITH VETERANS

Ignatius had atmosphere you could find nowhere else in the province. The school was intimately part of Chicago immigrant history. We scholastics mingled with history-makers. When a fire broke out in the rear section, we were told, one of the old-timers cried out. "Not the new wing!" referring to the 1895 construction. Buddy Esmaker, so called for his calling everyone Buddy, had retired from decades of teaching freshman Latin the year before I arrived. He shuffled around, fastening a gimlet eye on one and all.

Ray Grant had been the fire-breathing principal in the 40s and earlier 50s. I found him kindly and alert, a splendid individual. On Sundays I drew my assignment now and then to go with him to the nearby juvenile detention center, the Audy Home, where he said mass for the inmates. With them he was gruff but no more so than he'd been with students, I supposed.

Father Grant's secretary was Brother Mike O'Connor, who served long enough in the position for the quip to gain currency, "Who's buried in Grant's tomb? Brother O'Connor."

Ignatius and next-door Holy Family church were at the heart of Irish immigration. My grandparents James H. and Mary Clarke Bowman, he from Kingston, Ontario, she from County Mayo, wed at Holy Family in 1883. My father, Paul Clarke Bowman, and my mother,

Kathryn O'Connell, wed at St. Thomas Aquinas, five miles to the west, in 1919. The youngest of my three brothers and my sister were married at St. Catherine of Siena, a mile west of that, in 1950 and 1962. Thus went the migration. But Ignatius stayed.

James H. Bowman watched the 1871 Chicago fire from his back yard, I was told—at Jefferson and Harrison, according to his 1935 Chicago Herald Examiner obituary. That's two blocks north of the O'Leary barn, where the fire started, then moved east and away from his house and Holy Family church and the two-year-old St. Ignatius. Miraculously, it was believed.

He might also have watched parades down Roosevelt Road, then 12th Street, of the temperance societies, a sure adjunct to the Irish neighborhood. Heading the marching abstainers, would be a crusading priest, followed by men and their wives and children. "Father, dear Father, come home with me now," sung plaintively by the drinker's small daughter in a saloon, was not merely a popular refrain. Something like it happened, often.

In any case, your average community of priests and brothers had its drink problem. It was still so in the 1950s. "Some of us drink too much," we of the Ignatius community were told (by one of us who didn't) in the Jesuit chapel in 1957, and a 25-year-old took note. I had learned to tell dry wine from sweet at West Baden and now, a fledgling teacher, was hearing how the veterans talked to each other.

The speaker, one of the community, knew whereof he spoke. Such confrontation was rare, however, no matter what Saints Paul and Ignatius had to say about correcting one's brother. We corrected each other regularly as novices, face to face or in a group, but not regularly or not at all as the years wore on. We had to live with each other, after all.

HOUSES OF NON-CORRECTION

In our era, decades later, there appears to be similar tolerance for the more publicized failing of sexual performance and predatory molestation. The Jesuits suffered a "gaying and graying" experience in the wake of the exodus from their ranks beginning in the '60s, say Peter McDonough and ex-Jesuit sociologist Eugene C. Bianchi in their 2002 book *Passionate Uncertainty: Inside the American Jesuits.*

The 2000 Kansas City Star series on priests dying of AIDS nailed Jesuits hard—and was judged in Jesuit-edited *America* as giving "plausible" figures but ones far lower than those among "highly sexually active gay populations," which some would consider beside the point. Indeed, the writer, a Jesuit medical doctor, blamed the Star for being late with old news about homosexual and AIDS-afflicted priests. His main point, however, was to emphasize tolerance and understanding of the sexually active.

Indeed, a mood and policy of acceptance seems to be the norm, and in-house critics such as Navy and Marine chaplain Paul Shaughnessy and publisher Joseph Fessio are few. If the spirit of the "exercitium modestiae," the in-the-round sessions where those with or without sin threw stones, ever endured beyond novitiate, it has not endured in recent years, to judge from published accounts.

To emphasize the gap further, if criticism of Jesuit drinking habits was rare in the '50s, criticism of their sexual habits was almost nonexistent. Sexual sin in general, forget homosexual, was what no one apparently dared name, though we scholastics joked about it, as I have mentioned. On one occasion we were hit hard on the subject, in an eight-day retreat given by a New Yorker, Vincent McCorry, who turned the Exercises into "Sexercises," I said at the time.

It was McCorry, an America Magazine columnist who wrote on spiritual matters, who produced two of the most dramatic moments in my Jesuit retreat-going. One was his Gothic portrayal of masturbation as kicking Jesus in the face during his final agonies. The other was his reading a note from one of us—this in the early 60s—raising problems encountered by the homosexuals among us. McCorry read it at a daily session just before lunch, in which he answered questions or discussed issues sent to him in writing during the retreat.

There were 200 or so of us in the main chapel at West Baden. We were a quiet group in church under any circumstances, chuckling maybe when the diminutive Brother Freddy turned his hearing aid up too high in the front row and a high humming sound resulted. But we were never quieter than when McCorry read the note from a homosexual among us, a cry for help.

McCorry gave his advice—sympathetic, if primitive—which included indulging one's artistic proclivities. How many of us thought immediately of extensive decorations of chapels by various sacristans over the years is anybody's guess. In any case, the McCorry intervention stood alone in my 18 years as a Chicago Province Jesuit in the 50s and 60s. The proclivity was never named.

FESTO ITALIANO

Teaching was rough going, as was common in one's first year; but the year ended well. The students, mostly south and west siders, were a good lot from whom you could learn things. From a Taylor Street Italian I heard the word "paisan" ("pie-zahn," accent on second syllable) used for "friend." It's related to the English "peasant."

It was also the title of a 1948 war movie. In my mind I spelled it "pyzon" and heard it used contemptuously by non-Italians. But young Caifano, a very good kid with the same last name as a prominent mobster, referred with a smile to his "paisano," meaning friend or at least countryman. You talked to people, you learned things.

Ignatius backed up on an alley just north of Taylor Street, Little Italy's Main Street. An eight-foot stone wall separated property and alley, enclosing a football practice field that had all the grass that one would expect to find in a vacant lot. The coach was Dr. Ralph Mailliard, "Mal," a math teacher who also coached track, at which the students were successful. He was much loved and appreciated, but by the mid-50s was much suspected of having lost that winning football touch.

His team's trademark surprise was a quick kick on third down, meant to throw the opposition into disarray as the punt sailed over their heads, depriving them of good field position but at the same time giving them the ball. The school gave up on football a few years later.

Holy Family Church next door to the school had a mostly Taylor Street Italian membership. There was Our Lady of Pompeii a few blocks west and north, a Giovanni-come-lately in that church-rich but increasingly worshiper-poor neighborhood. And there were St. Callistus and Notre Dame, which my grandmother, Kit O'Connell, called "the French church," to which for reasons of personal devotion she had a grandson take her years earlier.

Holy Family had the old-church flavor, its inside newly and garishly painted and full of small altars strewn throughout at which the school's many priests said separate, private masses every day, each with a scholastic as server, as early as 5:30 a.m. It was quite a way to begin one's teaching day in a huge drafty building on a cold winter morning. Years later came the "concelebration" option for priests—two or more saying mass together at one altar, the better to profit from the communal aspect of liturgy—the only way there was, reformers would be claiming.

STUDENT REVOLT

The year ended well, I say, but not before I'd had my share of classroom disturbance. That was my big problem, though our principal was also a problem for me. This was Rudy Knoepfle, who was new at the job, as I was new at mine. Classroom work was rough going, especially with my two sophomore sections, of four in all. The other two were freshmen. They were all boys, of course. Not for many years was Ignatius to go coed. When it did, in a moment in the school's history not foreseen by founding Father Arnold Damen, the principal stood in the pulpit of Holy Family church and informed the newly arrived girls that among other requirements they had to wear bras.

In 1957 we had other issues. Our students were rough and tumble, from Beverly on the far South Side, Taylor Street, Oak Park and even west suburban Hinsdale and points beyond and between. (The Hinsdale student had been given no choice in the matter by his alumnus father, as had others by their alumni fathers, to be sure.) One hundred parishes were represented. When those born outside the U.S. had to declare themselves to the immigration service, 100 did so, out of 1,000 or so students.

Years later, when Martin Luther King marched on the Southwest Side, when I was back teaching at Ignatius, students of mine jeered from the sidewalks while rocks flew, one of which felled the good doctor, as was widely reported. One student, who was black, was catching the rocks with a baseball mitt. Not that we had many blacks—almost none in 1957 and a scattering in 1965, a year or so before that march.

In 1957, I was having little of racial protest and counter-protest, however. My problem was heading off daily commotion in a roomful of 42 boys, though one of the roomfuls had only 36! The freshmen were cowed by the novelty of their circumstance and less buffeted by puberty's onslaught. The sophomores were not cowed and were all buffeted, I presumed.

I began to read more carefully what Jesus said about doves and serpents—about being wise as the latter, simple as the former—noting that he put the wise part first. Not for me, I hoped, was to be the lot of the scholastic in another school who reportedly told his room full of boys, "There are entirely too many people walking around here," when in the ordinary course there was supposed to be only one, himself.

I discussed my problem with a young priest assigned to the Ignatius community, a trained counselor who sometimes received clients at the school. He had the answer to my problem with unruly boys: slap them. I did, open hand front or back across face, or once a book on top of head, whatever it took to gain instant respect or that fear which looks a lot like it. Respect did not always follow, of course, though many of the boys seemed to see the rough justice of a blow if timed right and given only after warning.

The potential slapper could say, "That's enough. . . OK, quiet," approaching with a very serious look, and only when it was clear to the others that the kid, forewarned, was asking for it (or couldn't stop asking for it), slap him. Rudy Knoepfle was not happy with my discipline problems. Discussing the situation with him, I told of the slapping. "Strike a boy?" he said, incredulous. I told him who had recommended it. He looked away. They were both good men.

Knoepfle was right, of course, but it was clear that if I couldn't achieve order in the class, I was a goner, and it was a matter of them or me. How to do it was the question. Mostly decent kids they were, doing dumb things, but there was work to do, I figured.

Besides, I had the memory of Father Regan at Fenwick giving a quick slap to a lippy kid who wouldn't stop defending or excusing himself. It was in the hall between classes. Regan in his white robe would have been carrying his sheaf of papers in his left hand. The kid was stunned but hardly hurt: it was quick and accurate. He got the message and shut up. Fenwick was not known for hitting kids, however. Neither was Ignatius, and Knoepfle was shocked to hear of it. Later, as a priest teacher, I didn't do it, though once I shoved a kid.

The trouble was mostly in my first few months at Ignatius. By year end, when a cherry bomb went off in the library, where I was monitoring a study period, I had a better grip on things. With great deliberation, I had one student shut the door, which meant I had the culprit in hand if I could distinguish him from the other 60 or so, which was impossible, I knew. I had another student take names. It was dumbshow. I was not about to jug the 60. I had not even a small chance of nailing the guilty one. He had covered his tracks. Main thing is, I did not get excited.

It helped too that these Ignatius kids were not out to subvert me but to have fun, as with the cute-little-archer "Bud Bowman" sign, a Bowman Dairy point-of-sale cutout four feet high, which I encountered in the library stacks during another study period. I had to laugh, of course. Indeed, by later in the year, I could stand in

the gym next to bleachers at a basketball game with a bunch of my
students and enjoy it. It was the likes of these who had put up the
Bud Bowman sign.

The Beverly-mostly-Irish and Taylor Street-mostly-Italian division
was something to consider, however. The Taylor Street boys generally
did not get with the program, as in extracurricular activities, except
to come to class and get the prized diploma. The Beverly Irish were
mostly on top of things, involved. I gathered that I was seen by
the paisanos as favoring the Irish. This could have been because I
enjoyed them. One of them flinched in the seat in front of me as I
raised my hand to make a point. He meant it too. I had nothing of
the sort in mind. I stopped and looked at him quizzically. A very
funny moment.

On the other hand, a Holy Family boy whose growth spurt had given
him a man's appearance as a sophomore was delighted to read for
my class his first book. It was one I might have read as a seventh-
grader, but the more satisfaction was in it for me the teacher. I
cherish that memory, but the divide was there. Another paisano told
a teacher he had two ways of talking, on the street and at Ignatius.
Knowing the difference, he was able to manage in two worlds.

A few years later, in the mid-60s, when I was at Ignatius as a priest,
I accompanied another former student one summer afternoon into a
Taylor Street bar. We had a beer and I got hard looks from one or
more patrons who knew me not only to be a priest but also as the
priest who spent time on the other side of Roosevelt Road with "the
coloreds." In his view, I had chosen my side, and it wasn't theirs.

CHANGE OF VENUE

In any case, if by the close of first year I had got the hang of running a class and managing passably well with the boys, I had been too clearly seen as suffering under Rudy Knoepfle, "the terrible Teuton," as one scholastic called him. In this, Rudy's first year as a principal and my first as a teacher, he did not approve of my performance and showed it, and I chafed under his tutelage. I probably hinted at the situation to the provincial in my conference with him at the time of his mid-year "visitation," as we called it.

In any case, when province assignments were posted in the spring, I was scheduled for Loyola Academy, in Wilmette, where Tom Murray, the soul of ease and professionalism, was in his umteenth year as a principal. I was apparently expected to fare better there. Murray, a big relaxed guy, was perfect for a supposed bruised reed like me. He gave me classes full of students who were amazingly ready to learn.

I slapped a senior on my first day, barely grazing him, and got a very helpful reputation from that. I relaxed in suburban surroundings and was pretty much off to the races. A year later, who should arrive at Loyola but the terrible Teuton himself, Knoepfle. But by then I had some seasoning and was ready to respond to his heavy hand on the tiller, which he naturally eased up on as a result.

At Loyola I began pushing the racial business in addition to my English teaching, and that didn't always go well. I had my students read Twain's *Puddn'head Wilson*, a story of black and white babies switched at birth, and emphasized the racial angle, banging it home. Not for many years did it dawn on me that I'd been something of a scold.

Nobody likes one, but scolding is out of place, I realized, especially in the classroom, which is for engaging mind and heart but mainly mind, trying to help students make it in a mindless world. Instead, I injected tension into the learning situation—not always a bad thing, to be sure—beyond what was helpful. A more muted presentation would have done better. Those who were receptive would have got the point. The others would have squirmed but got it later.

I had other ways to push various agenda—assigning compositions about labor unions, for instance. One father said I had objected to the kid's composition because he disagreed with me. The father argued the point well in conversation at a fathers' club gathering. You were more likely to run into that at Loyola than Ignatius, where parents' educational level was a step or two lower and comments were earthier. One Ignatius father, for instance, told one of us about his son, an exemplary student, that he "wouldn't say shit if he had a mouthful." The boy later joined the Jesuits, staying several years, and had a distinguished newspaper and authorial career.

Another Ignatius father dispatched traffic for a trucker. Another, whom I knew from errand-boy days as a high-schooler, ran an electrotype machine. Loyola parents, on the other hand, were more likely to be upper-level managers, business owners, even socialites. One kid, a big and good-natured senior, rode his horse onto the campus at lunch time on a spring day just before graduation, when seniors had the day off. I can still see him galloping across the football field. There was of course the vast middle in each school that was transferable. But that didn't change the overall dynamic.

The Loyola kids were less direct, more politic and more devious. The study-period cherry bomb at Ignatius had as its counterpart the senior lounge roar during lunch period, with lights out and an attempt to ignite my cassock, for God's sake. Nasty stuff, as if there were more pent-up hostility there and less awareness of what happens to bad guys if they don't watch out. Father Charley Conroy, a young priest faculty member, appeared just in time at the lounge door and stopped it all pronto. Charley, later a chaplain in Viet Nam, had authority that I lacked. That attempted lighting up of my cassock was in a class by itself.

Later, teaching at Ignatius as a priest, I fielded questions that never would have been asked at Loyola, such as one from a Bohemian-ancestry senior about "this 'bohemian' business" after a character in a short story spoke of being bohemian, meaning artistic, as a lifestyle choice. He was genuinely puzzled. Answer a question like that, you feel you've pushed ignorance back visibly and maybe headed off a bar fight at some future date.

On the other hand, Bill Daley, Mayor Richard J. Daley's youngest son, later secretary of commerce, Al Gore campaign manager, and Obama White House chief of staff, asked why the short stories we were reading all had unhappy endings. It was something we might have spent a semester on but didn't—one of those teaching moments that I let slip away.

Ignatius was a rich environment and satisfying in its way. But as a scholastic in the late '50s, it was at Loyola where I found students I could run with. Tom Murray gave me classes of higher literacy than I'd had at Ignatius. A year later Murray was gone, and Rudy Knoepfle came to Loyola as principal, moving from Ignatius as part of the new rector's plan for saving the Academy, as I saw it at the time.

FORT LARAMIE

The academy had moved in 1957 from Rogers Park on the Loyola University campus to a new Wilmette campus bordering the Edens expressway on the west. It had a Laramie Avenue address, the same

Laramie that runs through the West Side a mile east of Oak Park. The building sat in splendid isolation on the space of two or more city blocks. Charley Conroy called it Fort Laramie.

The building, a cement-block construction on two floors, was no architectural gem. One scholastic called it a button factory. But it had lots of space for athletic fields and team practices, a big gym (whose floor buckled zanily shortly after installation), and a great swimming pool. Jesuit living quarters included a top-floor scholastics' rec room and a first-floor fathers' rec room, rather nicely appointed, leather-cushioned chairs and all, at first out of bounds for scholastics, later not.

We had privacy, unlike in the ancient Ignatius building, where you could walk out of your bedroom into the hall right outside the rickety gymnasium. One scholastic had a narrow room under the stairs. High windows opened on to Roosevelt Road, then served by electric trolley buses—now and then a bus went off its trolley, and the driver had to get off and reconnect it, by hand. We looked out on so-called ABLA Homes—Abbott, Brooks, Loomis, (Jane) Addams—a multi-building housing project or group of projects that stretched a half mile west and east.

At Loyola there were no rooms under staircases, nor partly brick-paved Roosevelt Road or housing project or trolleys, just the Edens Expressway a half-block away on one side and the pleasant streets of Northfield to the west, with the length of several football fields on the south. Very suburban. But the place was going under. The Knights of Columbus were on the verge of calling their loan, we heard, at which point a nice big button factory would go on the market and Loyola would disappear.

At the helm of this institution as its rector was the nicest, least offensive guy who ever oversaw a debacle of such magnitude. He had come with the new building, might have been in on its construction. Whether he was or not, once at the helm he was in over his head, and Fort Laramie was sinking in the sands of west Wilmette. He made sure no lights were left lit at night. We Jesuits ate fish on Friday that was bought cheap by the boatload. Economy was the byword. None of it mattered. The Knights were closing in.

A year into my time at Loyola, the province fathers reached into their store of talent and came up with a Chicago Irishman named English, ranking Jesuit at the Loyola University dental school and before that a high-ranking Army chaplain during the world war that had ended 13 years previously. Mike English was smart, charming, personable, and above all realistic about the jam we were in. He told someone that as rector it was the first time in his 30-plus years in the Jesuits that he wasn't sleeping at night.

His predecessor went back to Cincinnati to resume his quiet life as a kindly priest and low-level administrator. Mike English was installed as rector. The usual term was six years. The other man had lasted two, which is as good a measure as any of how serious the situation was. When you remove a rector after two years, something is up.

THE ENGLISH ERA

Mike English brought John Reinke with him. Reinke was a psychological counselor and piano player, a handsome, smart guy who could wow an audience. The salesman factor went double for English, who had the most direct, no-nonsense manner of all superiors I ever had. He also acquired Rudy Knoepfle, much as a new coach acquires assistants. Tom Murray went elsewhere, eventually if not then to Cincinnati's St. Xavier High School, where to my considerable benefit I ran into him some years later.

Why Knoepfle? Because he was in his way a hot shot, and English wanted the hottest shots around. In addition, Knoepfle may have ruffled too many feathers at the more tradition-minded Ignatius. These things are rarely simple. And straight-talking Tom Murray may have sensed high-level salesmanship on the horizon and wasn't interested.

Leaving Ignatius with me in 1958 had been Florian, "Zim," Zimecki, a veteran Latin teacher with a remedial-reading specialty, torn from his comfort-providing Ignatius and sent or exiled to distant Loyola. Knoepfle may have called the shot on that one, as he may have called it on me, for that matter. Zim consoled himself with reference to the swimming pool, which he intended to use as a weight-control measure but never did that I could tell. He got back to Ignatius eventually; so all ended comparatively well for him.

English's task was to make a go of a school in danger of going under, in the service of "the church," as he put it. This was the first time I heard of my life's work, my vocation, expressed in this manner. It had been in the service of Christ the King, which gave it a collective tinge, since kings had kingdoms, but was essentially a personal matter between me and Christ, whose kingdom was not of this world. He said so himself, didn't he? We said Christ, not Jesus, in those days, before ecumenical, especially interfaith, considerations led us to downplay him as Messiah by calling him simply Jesus.

Focus was on conscience and duty. We were to give our all as soldiers of Christ, compromising nowhere. In effect we had imbibed a reformist mentality, and for those who caught the radical, even anarchic, element in all that, the institutional church was a potential hindrance. We were saved from heresy by obedience, each calling on himself as a stick in an old man's hand, to quote St. Ignatius, again as a personal matter. But resting in the bosom of mother church, we were nonetheless vipers at the ready, critical and detached, a sort of cabal.

Not Mike English, who if he ever nourished such considerations did not show it. We younger Jesuits were said to think that each had the Holy Spirit to guide him individually, as opposed to church authority, its divinely licensed leadership, whose guidance should have been enough for us. We did think that way. We thought each had the Spirit, whom we had got at confirmation and had been relying on ever since. So did Martin Luther, and there you had a problem.

In addition, as young men we were naturally alert to institutional failings. It's what young men do, after all. But English talked of serving the church, which he did not envision as ethereal. On the contrary, it was something that called for bricks and mortar if it was to achieve its goals. In this case it called for the salvation of Loyola Academy.

In this cause it was a pleasure to work under someone who seemed to know what he was doing, especially one who appreciated producers. English would introduce us scholastics at a reception for Jesuit family members, citing our achievements, and paid attention in other ways. When his man Reinke came down to Baden a few years later, several of us former teachers at Loyola, now theologians, gathered with him. By then we were students, passive recipients of other people's instruction and feeling at times lower than whale droppings. Working for English, one did not feel like whale dropping.

The same went for Knoepfle. In 1959, my third year teaching and the year he arrived at Loyola, he was a better principal after two years on the job, and I was a better teacher. If I put my students to studying vocabulary, ten words a day from a paperback book, and told him the purpose was to make them more aware of words rather than merely pick up ten words a day, he took it seriously and quoted me.

The scholastic didn't always get that kind of respect. When a veteran Jesuit teacher spotted a collection of student writings that I left out in the rec room for all to see, he grunted and flipped it back on the table. When Knoepfle died in spring of my last year teaching, I lost one of my reasons for doing a good job.

RACE BECAME AN ISSUE

Meanwhile, as a teacher I had my assigned "sodality" work with students as my extracurricular responsibility. The sodality—"of Our Lady"—was a student organization meant to promote religious devotion. That meant daily prayer and self-examination presumably inspired by one-on-one conferences with the Jesuit moderator and "closed" group retreats at a retreat house. It was thankless work for the most part, though some students may have derived profit from it, and in any case it was a show of personal interest in them that they would have noticed.

There had been nothing like it at Fenwick, where Dominicans were less aggressive, even shy about it, and reaped far fewer recruits. We Jesuits took kids in hand and taught them what we knew, especially scholastics—a breed of cat not teaching at Fenwick. Nor was the sodality a fringe organization. It had 40 or 50 members in each school year, including athletes and school leaders. I had the juniors.

We worked on their spirituality, as we called it, but also on "apostolic" work, the so-called apostolate, which we identified in old-fashioned works of mercy. Sodalists visited old folks and orphans, packed and delivered food for the needy at Christmas time, and performed other good deeds—works of mercy, as I say, using the phrase that preceded transformation of society as the accepted goal for church workers.

There were spiritual and corporal works of mercy. We had learned about them in the catechism as kids, long before societal goals and the pursuit of social justice became the norm. Ahead of the curve, I made "racial justice" my specialty, bringing Sodalists to visit black people and hear lectures and in general have their consciousness raised in matters of interracial concern.

MY NEGRO PROBLEM

Race became my focus. It was a time when Marillac House on the West Side, a Daughters of Charity settlement house, lost donors when its clientele went black.

Patrick Crowley, an Irishman of unfailing politesse, resigned from the Chicago Athletic Association, the Michigan Avenue bastion of Irish prosperity to which my grandfather and uncle had belonged and my brother would belong, because he couldn't bring his colored friends there. Instead he joined a new club atop the nearby new Prudential Building, which at 35 floors was Chicago's tallest.

The Chicago Serra Club, dedicated to fostering religious vocations, lost a whole meeting debating whether to admit a black member. I heard about it from my father, who was to introduce the day's speaker, Father Jim Egan, a Jesuit living at Ignatius who worked with deaf mutes. It was a Friday lunch in a Loop hotel such as my father attended for years, coming to our dinner table at night enthusiastic about nuggets of Catholic teaching he had never got in his two years of Catholic grade school. The then-famous Father Patrick Peyton spoke there, and we as a family began saying the rosary.

Jim Egan was a little guy, red-faced and near-sighted with a permanent backward tilt to his head as if from a lifetime of looking up to talk to people, which he did at the drop of a hat, his face wreathed in smiles.

You knew when he had his mutes for basketball in the Ignatius gym, across the hall from Jesuit quarters, from the grunts and moans that accompanied their play. When you're in the clear and the guy with the ball doesn't see you and you can't talk, you do what you can to get his attention.

But there was no hearing from Jim Egan on the day a point of disorder was raised by an intensely anti-black member, a county judge, who vociferously objected to a proposed Negro or "colored" member. The whole business left my father sick to his stomach, as I remember he had felt after we overheard anti-semitic remarks from another restaurant table many years before. Jimmy Egan had to be rescheduled for Serra.

In that climate, I mounted forays into black neighborhoods under auspices of Friendship House, bringing sodalists with me. This caught the attention of people trying to save Loyola from the Knights of Columbus. I know this from hearing it months later, not from admonitions by Mike English, who never objected. English could hear about it and be aware of a Bowman reputation stemming from it and say nothing to Bowman about it. Never once was I told not to push interracialism. Never once did superiors try to stop me, then or later. How ridiculous would sound to me the ex-priests who said they left the ministry because of racism.

Later, as a priest teaching at Ignatius in the mid-60s, I pressed racial issues very hard and reported to a meeting of Chicago-area teachers what I was doing. Many were amazed that I got away with it. In public schools, for instance, they had no such license to push the issue. But in our Catholic school, I had church teaching and my priestly authority to back me up.

So at Loyola Academy in the late 50s, when on a Saturday morning other scholastics were out with debaters at a tournament or various teams at games, I was going to the South Side or downtown Chicago with my charges. After one busy weekend at this sort of thing, I turned up sick Monday morning, and a classmate had to cover for me. I got reminded of that for some time. There was Bowman getting all excited about justice but unable to teach his classes.

My racial preference sent me to Mike English on the day of the entrance exam in January, 1960, as my last Loyola semester began. A black kid had come for the test, and the assistant principal, as if to settle our fears, told one of us the kid wouldn't make it whatever his score. I went for English, who did not deny it, said it would "hurt us" to take the kid. In a few years we could afford to do so, he said.

It was an awful revelation, but English didn't soft-soap me. There was in him none of the excited concern I caught from others over the years. English knew I could make a stink about it (I didn't) but said nothing about this. He also knew he had a make-or-break financial situation on his hands as regards the academy and the example of Marillac House and its disappearing contributors. In any event, he was straight about it, which is rare enough among administrators.

Without palaver about being a team player—it was not the point and he was too smart to make it—he just laid out the situation. Later I told an older Jesuit about our meeting. He advised that it was nothing to leave the Jesuits about. I agreed, mainly because of my commitment but also because I liked Mike English.

CLOSET SKELETONS

But a few years later, in a worse matter, English's sidekick John Reinke as rector did what dozens of church leaders did in misreading predators' threat. His "Dear Don" letter in January of 1970—"I've made a dozen attempts to write this," he began—almost apologetically informed Donald McGuire that he would have to leave Loyola, this in the wake of a letter six weeks earlier from a North Side pastor relaying to Reinke what a parishioner, a Loyola student, said about being abused by McGuire. McGuire left Loyola for other pastoral work but years later was accused, tried, and found guilty in state and federal courts for crimes of sexual abuse committed against Loyola students and other boys.

Loyola Academy was also home, during my time there, to Wilton Skiffington, a wiry, uncommunicative fellow 20 years my senior, who became the subject of law suits in 2003, 15 years after his death, when he was exposed post mortem in steamy letters he had written to a student whom he had apparently abused beginning when the boy was 15.

In addition, John Powell, seven years ahead of me in the society, became the subject of a number of abuse suits initiated by Loyola University coeds. Powell taught at Loyola U. and also wrote enormously successful spiritual books and was accordingly praised and respected. Among his supporters was the ascetical, even saintly, John Hardon, who had taught Powell at West Baden and found him "very gifted" and possessing "a good mind," one who "could write well." (This in an undated essay, "To Rechristianize America," published on the web site of the Real Presence Association.) It's a measure of how good Powell looked to others before his exposure.

THE MOTHER TONGUE

All was not social-problem-solving for me as a teacher, however. There was ever the classroom, of course, and the delicious prospect of leading a roomful of boys to first place in the regional province exams. These were taken, all on one day, at a dozen Jesuit high schools in the middle part of the U.S., including the New Orleans-based Southern Province. We believed in competition and made no bones about it. You had to pass an entrance exam to get into a Jesuit school, and once in, you were grouped in A, B, C, etc. classes, top to bottom based on scores, no apologies given. Schools congratulated themselves on the height of their cutoff point, and still do, competing even now for the more promising students.

It was a sort of stock price: the better your students tested, the higher your stock. This was the Jesuit way, at Loyola and Ignatius, as it was the Dominican way at Fenwick and the Carmelite way at Mt. Carmel High, on the South Side. So it was that the four Chicago-area high schools run by these three orders wanted their own days for entrance exams, fearing the effect on enrollment of a common exam day.

These were days when many parents cared passionately about getting their kids into Catholic schools, and not just because public schools were lesser opportunities. If a boy was unsure of passing the test, he was wise to take a placement exam for a Christian Brothers school or other school committed to serve the general population. Call it elitism, or better, merit-based selection.

In the desperate days of 1959, on the other hand, exceptions to the selectivity model were made at Loyola, where students were needed to fill seats in empty classrooms. Mike English instituted a 1-K section, lower even than 1-J, for kids who would not have made it into Loyola but had money for tuition. The school's existence was at stake: it was time for a fine-tuned departure from the Jesuit model, if not a dipping of the flag.

The also-rans were not for me, however. By this third year of my teaching, 1959–60, back under Knoepfle as principal and with the English-Reinke team at the helm, I was assigned A, B, and C classes, freshmen and sophomores, it being decided, apparently, that there was more bang to be gotten from the buck this way from Bowman, who was big on reading and writing but less so on discipline, or classroom management, which for these students was a minor issue. For me, therefore, were sections that moved briskly along. The boys came from families where reading was taken for granted. All had well above the minimum requirement for the reading habit. They were ready for the academic varsity.

The Jesuit high school writing series, by a Jesuit in Dallas, was very helpful. Freshman and sophomores used *Correct Writing* and *Adult Writing* respectively, about writing the sentence and the paragraph respectively. The books presented an orderly approach, offering dozens of rules, examples, and exercises. A four-year brown-cover handbook was eminently citable. In it each rule was tagged with letter and number. We went over them so often, I could just scribble F-11 on a paper, and the student would know it meant his sentence wandered without focus. As a writer I have thanked my stars that I taught freshman and sophomore English to such students out of such a book. It made me a copy editor for life.

The literature book—too big, too heavy, too expensive, and not especially imaginative—was something else. We turned to paperbacks—cheap, packable in a hip pocket, offering an unlimited store of reading to match each boy's capacity and interests. Boys could pack a book in a hip pocket, have it ready any time. It was literacy on the go. I'd order a supply of books from the school book store, and they'd be ready in a week for assigned reading by all.

IN THE CLASSROOM

The paperback option permitted me to assign books as the year progressed, gauging student progress and acting to suit. For paperbacks at low rates, I had the book store. But I also had school and public libraries. Every kid had to get a public library card. The book store became a fall-back option. Better they got the book out of a library, because it could be habit-forming, I figured. One student lived in an unincorporated area near Winnetka and had to make do somehow as to libraries. But it's a land of public libraries, and my requirement got boys to darken their doors at least for the time it took to get a card.

Note that I had authority in the matter: they cared how well they did, their parents cared, they built on previous experience. We were in step with each other. Even the burly St. Ignatius student who read his first book as a sophomore had not been so culturally determined as to shrug his shoulders at the possibility.

Taylor Street was rough and ready, but it did not penalize reading. The paisano kid was not worried about acting Irish a la Beverly, as black kids worry about acting white, or defiantly reject the concept. This is a case for black kids of overcoming their environment. We all have to do that, one way or another, picking and choosing what we keep, negotiating within ourselves with the impulses and instincts we grow up with. Taking self-ownership, you might say. With a little luck, we come to terms in the matter. Or don't.

At Loyola my students read books I assigned on which they were tested for content-absorption. And they read books of their own choosing, for which I gave extra credit if they could show they had read it well enough to answer my quick questions about it at my desk at the end of the school day. They knew where to find me and could come by in the 15 minutes or so after the final bell, hand me the book, at which I gave a quick look, figuring out a few main fact-oriented questions on the spot.

There were no book reports, just reading and remembering a

reasonable amount of what was read. Neither were there book reports for assigned books: I'd quiz them 100 pages at a time, a series of five quick questions every few days as they read assigned pages, all fact-based, again the sort of thing they could be expected to know. The answers were short, on half sheets of paper. I could mark the quizzes in a jiffy that night, return them the next day. This was important so that each would have a record of how he was doing and have regular reminders of the quizzes' importance. He'd know right away in fact, when we worked over the five questions just asked.

Here's where the iron was struck while hot. Discussion focused on the immediate issue of whether the kid got the answer right or wrong. They would grin or grimace as they learned the right answer. Sometimes they argued their case. If the argument was good enough, I'd concede. Those arguments were worth it, allowing us all to have our say, including me. These were great moments with kids who knew how to read the material at hand and cared about what they read.

I assigned no book reports, as I said. They had been the bane of my existence as a student, when I would groan at hearing friend Bill brag about writing one in 47 minutes. Mine would take days, as I told too much about the book, which I had loved reading but got all tied up writing about.

I wanted my students to write, of course. They did a composition a week, often based on the book being read, so that they could react (with evidence) to what they were reading without writing a review as such, which is something proven writers get paid for regularly. These were unproven writers getting the hang of it. I was looking for sentences and paragraphs that made sense and were spelled right and had decent syntax and due respect for data.

I also told them how long they should write, say 300 to 500 words. I did not want them to kiss off the assignment, nor did I want them to ramble. I was not interested in someone's slapdash, loosely constructed life story. Some could write long and not waste words, but most could not. On the other hand, if one of them pulled it off, I did not complain.

Correcting the essays, I would bleed all over the sheet with my red ballpoint, often using proofreading marks supplied by the brown handbook. Such a series this was, one of Loyola University Press's finest. It was dropped years later at Loyola and probably in other Jesuit schools—"change for the sake of change," one of my former students, then an English teacher at Loyola, told me. A shame.

The amount of red marking had nothing to do with the grade of a given composition. I once showed a two- or three-pager to the class with as much red as typescript, to which I gave an A+ for its intelligence and overall excellence but also because it was venturesome and detailed and gave me much to comment on, even to correct. The writer got his money's worth, I told the class. His parents' money, that is.

Compositions were due on Friday. I returned them on Monday. We discussed them then. There was much discussion, with plenty of opportunity for me to drive home various writing principles. Getting quizzes and papers back pronto was of the essence. It was important they knew their mistakes early, so as to avoid them next time around. This was writing to learn how to write, not to pass a test.

THE GOLD

I pitched the province exams hard. "Eye hath not seen nor ear heard, nor hath it entered into the mind of man, to imagine what I have prepared for you if you win the province exams," I told 2-A, adapting Scripture to my purpose. They took the challenge. They studied and I drilled, using readily available former exams, and tested and quizzed.

This getting ready for a test can be a teaching device. That is, a learning device. What does the lawyer do when preparing for trial but bone up on data and burn them into his conscious and subconscious? Or the executive for a meeting? Or preacher for sermon or writer for writing a book? Or, for that matter, the boxer for a fight or quarterback before a game? It's performing under pressure. Schooling should include this, I say. If it's a good test, why not teach to it? It's excellent motivation for the schoolboy.

Your students have to be game for it, of course. They need a certain competence and confidence. You can't give that to someone, but you can encourage what's there and watch it grow. I had it as a kid. In sixth grade Sister Monica told me I was sure of myself. It was the first time I'd heard of being sure of myself as a good thing. I was encouraged at home and felt appreciated from my earliest days, but it was largely unspoken. It was good to hear at age 10 or 11 that it's good to be confident. It's where a teacher comes in.

My province-exam promise, put up on the blackboard, became a byword. In time I specified: win first place and no written homework the rest of the year, meaning exercise work, not compositions, but unfortunately without making that clear. Lesson: make EVERYTHING clear. And make no unfillable promises.

November became December, which became January, which got to its late days and brought the day and hour of the exam. The tests arrived on the day itself—freshman English, sophomore English, etc. through all levels and subjects. When they were taken, all on the same day, of course, they were sealed and sent to a Jesuit office in another state for correcting.

One morning the scores came back. I left 2A to walk downstairs to the principal's office to get the results. I walked back up and silently walked to the board, where I wrote "Province exam results, English, 1960. Loyola Academy 2-A, FIRST PLACE!" Their yell resounded through the silent halls. Such a day. It was their victory but mine too.

STRUGGLING

Meanwhile, there was the vocation-perseverance matter, still an annoyance no matter how many firsts my students won. I worked at dwelling on the good things I had in the most everyday sense possible, as in the good times with my confreres—not a bad stopgap measure. I had an out, of course: the church could dissolve my vows.

Absorption in the work at hand was another good tactic, not that I had a choice as a busy teacher, which I intended to be whatever else was going on inside my head. On the other hand, it didn't help any to go full speed ahead and get all tired out. We lived where we worked, and I wasn't always smart about using myself. Later, when Daily News columnist Mike Royko caught me working late in the city room on a story and observed that I hadn't worked that hard in my previous life, I said that had been the problem, or a problem: I had burned holy candles at both ends.

In any case, when a doctor suggested vitamin shots in my second year teaching, I took him up on the idea. They were the color of darkened orange juice, from a big fat syringe. I took them from him regularly for several months until the doc told me they were expensive, meaning I ought to call them off, which I did. Knowing Jesuits, he was pretty sure I wasn't thinking in terms of cost. However hard I was working and however tired I was getting, I was budgeting nothing. Mike English was doing our budgeting for us.

Doing my own budgeting had no appeal. Discussing options with a classmate a few years later, I said I couldn't see "chasing a buck" as a non-Jesuit. This would have struck the insomniac, financially pressured English as precious indeed. For most of us, freedom from financial worry was one of our perks. It came largely from not having wife and family to worry about. We were spared that, and with it unfortunately, the potential maturing effect that goes with it.

We scholastics had good times together, true. But it was no fun not having female friends or the freedom to slug beers on Saturday night and sleep in on Sunday morning, though our clean living in those early years had to be a contributor to physical health. We got up early, and to this day I have early morning habits.

Reminding myself of those good times, the brotherhood we enjoyed, ranked high among crass motives I used to buck myself up—crass as compared to the high-flying, all-for-Christ-the-king motivation we had nourished as novices. Walking alone in the school's neighborhood on a Chrismastime evening, seeing lights of comfortable homes and envying their inhabitants, I concentrated on my own good times. Thus consoled, I headed back to Fort Laramie for litanies and the night meal. It was not quite a whole-burnt offering, but it did for the moment.

My struggle was hardly heroic. The appeal was still there of the spiritual-idealistic and intellectual life. I was on the high road and reaped the psychic rewards of knowing it. Besides, everyone had his problems, I had to tell myself. As to this, it helped to get around, as to a late-night visit with fellow scholastic Pete Fox to the house of a friend of mine. This was Jack, a friendly, smart guy with a Rogers Park flair who had played basketball for Loyola Academy. He and his wife had six young kids. He was in television ad sales and moved with assurance in that fast-moving milieu.

He and Pete and I had a beer in his panelled basement. A word or two about Pete. As I mentioned before, he had gotten polio in our first few months at West Baden. Thereafter, he spent months in an iron lung, or tank respirator, in a Louisville hospital, where we took turns staying with him. Pete smoked too, contrary to Jesuit regs, and once showed a visitor how he could take in a drag while iron-lunging it and eventually expel it. A good story that.

In the novitate he had grown a plant next to his dormitory desk; and when Bill Dietrich, an older guy from Cleveland a year ahead of us and a Navy veteran, genially quizzed him on it, noting that the rules said no one was to have things others did not have, Pete, unfazed, said everyone should have a plant.

He had gotten polio after exploring a culvert beneath the front road at West Baden, we were told. He lost a year of training because of it, much of it spent at the hospital. At Loyola Academy, walking stiffly and with the potential of falling down if he wasn't careful, he taught math, for which he had a special talent. Low-key, witty, alert, Pete was someone my parents were always glad to have me bring along for a visit. His polio had knocked him out of athletics, at which he excelled, but he never complained. A splendid man.

My friend Jack and he were the sort to appreciate each other, each with his brand of earthy directness. In the course of the visit, Jack pointed out somewhat wistfully a keepsake that had been broken when one of his kids had knocked it over. Pete caught that and later noted that this sort of interruption was not ours as celibates to put up with. Without acrimony he could note the fussiness that characterized some of us and threatened us all as holy bachelors.

THE WORLD

We had our blood families, of course. I would go to the family home on Lombard Avenue for Thanksgiving, Christmas, and the like, often getting picked up by my father. From Ignatius I was more likely to hop a westbound Roosevelt bus or take the "L." I'd reach the latter via the Blue Island Avenue bus , a 10- or 15-minute ride to the Loop. This was before the Eisenhower Expressway median-strip train; but Ignatius was nonetheless in the center of things, via bus or rapid transit. From Wilmette, however, we travelled only by car.

As Jesuit parents mine had me to themselves more than they had their two married sons. Sometimes I would accompany them to visit their friends. Again, a married or even non-religious bachelor son would probably not have been taken along. I had left home at 18 and not returned for five years, but after seven years out of the house, I was a regular, happily and proudly exhibited by the mother and father. A few years later, as a priest stationed at Ignatius, I once took a call from my mother complaining that they hadn't seen me for a while. I belonged to them more as a Jesuit than if I'd not been one. Not so with my brother in Peru, nor would it have been so with me if I had gone to Nepal. Posted to Chicago, I was fair game for parental concern, no matter my age.

Not that I resisted. Home for Thanksgiving in 1959, my third year teaching and second under Rudy Knoepfle, I made a two-fer of it by going out to Oak Park also on the weekend. Always with permission of the minister, of course. We would enter his office and ask, Father-may-I? And Father would almost always say yes, but sometimes with a sidelong look that said volumes. You could take it seriously, or you could shrug it off; but you didn't tell him to knock it off. You probably should have called him on it: If you don't want me to do it, say so. But you didn't. One way or the other, you had to deal with it.

For instance, as a priest living at Ignatius in the summer after ordination, I negotiated with the minister for my travel to New England for tertianship, my final year of training. I wanted to go by way of New York, where I would stay for one or two nights at a midtown Manhattan Jesuit residence. "Two hundred dollars [or some such amount] for a vacation," said the minister, telling me that So&So had made the New York trip by bus.

Abashed but not enough to make me scratch my trip—I had to go east in any case—I took a plane and in New York saw a Broadway show with Jack Lucal, a Chicagoan stationed at this house, which housed the America Magazine staff. The show had a few risque moments. On our way out, in clerics of course, as one did routinely in those days, we got amused looks from fellow play-goers who did not know we were Jesuits seeking merely to broaden our experience. Nor did we explain.

DEATH

A few weeks after the 1959 Thanksgiving, I went to Lombard Avenue again, and Rudy Knoepfle said something to Mike English, who called me in, embarrassed by the need to interfere. When I said I'd not been "home" since Thanksgiving—it was almost Christmas—he was surprised. It was the sort of interaction that could get in the way of more important things for English, like saving Loyola; and it developed directly from our situation as presumably poor and obedient men, bound by vows. Rather, it developed from our unwillingness to make the superior (the boss) get specific about what he wanted, to clear the air, much as employees deal with bosses all over. We were supposed to fear nothing. Confident Christian candor was to be the norm. Or so I thought at the time, without acting on that conviction.

None of it mattered a few months later, when on the day after Easter, Rudy Knoepfle was found dead in his bed. The last I had seen of him, hours earlier, he had wished me a nice time with my parents as I made my way out the front door to get into my father's car. He said it with a genuine, soft manner, of which I took note.

The next I saw of him, he was flopped on his bed with the door open, which I noticed as I passed his room that night. He had his ways of doing things which I respected, and I passed without knocking. If Rudy Knoepfle wanted to sleep with his clothes on and the door open, it was his business, I thought. Next thing I knew of him was from the minister, expressionless, walking down the hall toward a group of us after breakfast, saying, "It's over," meaning the life of Rudy Knoepfle.

We waked him at the school. It was the closest I had been to sudden death or any other kind, for that matter. My maternal grandmother, the only grandparent I knew, had died when I was 14 or so, but

I have no recollection of being moved by that. With Knoepfle it was another story. With him gone, I said at the time, I had one less reason for doing a good job as a teacher.

A few months later, my regency ended, I was on a train headed back to West Baden for theology. I wanted just to finish theology, which I looked on as a necessary evil, and then get back to Loyola or another high school and pick up teaching where I'd left off. Ten years a Jesuit, at age 28, I was suffering career *interruptus* to be once more a full-time student.

CHAPTER 5. THEOLOGICAL QUESTIONS: THEOLOGY, 1960–1964

At the first it will be as welcome to thee as a prison,
and their very solutions will seem knots unto thee.
—Thomas Fuller on being a divinity student
in the 17th century

I returned to Baden, as I say, with my eye cast backwards on teaching. Theology was for being a priest, which had never had any great appeal for me. Rather, it was the Jesuit life that appealed: the order or orderliness of it, the academics, and now the teaching.

So it was a hard day in the life of this Jesuit when he returned from the fleshpots of regency to the halls of theology. I faced the grim alternative of life back at Baden, where I knew from experience I would have too much time to think and nobody to perform for but teachers, whom I had found a generally ungrateful lot. Nobody to do anything for and a big, faceless community to do it in.

I ended my first day with a short, quick breakdown in my room, lying abed before sleep, weeping. Then I rolled over and went to sleep. At 28 I had my life ahead of me, even if Baden was closing in.

REBELLION

I gritted my teeth and plunged in, making a splash. First, I locked horns with several teachers and the theology dean, who told me I was the most uncooperative theologian he had ever met. Of course. I hated it there. Pressured by him and facing some sort of dire punishment, I went to see two or three teachers and smoothed things over. But I did not see the chief complainer among them, a first-year teacher whom I'd known since I was in philosophy, he in theology. This fellow was of a rather tense disposition. Imagine that. He also probably felt under the gun, being new at teaching theologians, though not new at teaching fellow Jesuits. We had had him as a French teacher during juniorate summers. He did well by us, but this time it was another story.

He had me pegged for an intellectual in a highly abstracted mode, but I wasn't. I thought a lot but half the time was not in the infield where I belonged, fielding the sharply hit grounder with no time to think about it, but out in left field. Mine was not a scholarly temperament. He and I both absorbed a lot, but in him the absorbed tended to sort itself out. In me it went into a huge undifferentiated bushel basket from which it could be sucked up and worked over at random.

I saw connections but labored over systems. I looked for the imaginable. It had to make sense at first or second blush, or I got confused and then bored or panicked and then impatient or angry. This fellow's lucubrations about God left me wondering. I was having my Thomas Fuller experience: this fellow's solutions seemed like knots unto me.

He misread me, and he misread my friend Pat, whose shrewd intelligence was masked by taciturnity. When books were assigned, Pat got an easy book, I got a hard one, by a philosopher who was parsing the hell out of one or two words. I could not follow him. I read about 35 pages. I wrote about the 35 pages. The teacher was not pleased.

As for the dean, who had reports about me from him and other teachers, there was more at stake here than my adjustment to the pursuit of abstract theological questions. A young star had joined his faculty, and he had to back him up. He was adamant: I had to go see this star. I was apparently bothering him, and he was clearly bothering me. Something had to give.

Here was a new kind of crisis. I'd never been in defiance of anyone or accused of it. And now I faced the kind of confrontation that could undo ten years of putting up with things and interrupt my career or end it—an inglorious finish for one who once rejected rapine on the holocaust. I went into the chapel to sort it out.

I knelt down and asked myself, with God listening in, if I were to leave the Jesuits for greener pastures, was this how to go about it? Reacting to a tempest in a pot of tea? What would happen if I sat tight, declining to make it up with this fellow? Would I be rusticated, sent back to a high school for more teaching? Or defenestrated, told to find another line of work?

It was early enough in the school year for me to be put somewhere, in some school. The disgrace of it would have been nonexistent if I didn't feel it, and I would not have felt it. Nor, beyond some harmless gossip of the sort one can count on any time, anywhere, would there be a price to pay. The authorities liked me anyway, and thought I showed promise.

Besides, we were a big enough organization for a supposed misstep to go unnoticed or shrugged off. So what if I ran into a wall at Baden? There were a half dozen or more theology shops in the U.S. at the time. I might have started over at any one of them.

That wasn't the point anyhow. The point was commitment—the vows, for one thing, going back eight years, and what I promised in that Long Retreat, going back ten.

Whoa. One thing at a time, I decided. If I wanted to leave, commitment or not, let it not happen over this. I should clear up this matter. I should go and see the holdout teacher, eating crow. (Nothing else would do, I was convinced.) I went, and it turned out he had a number of bones to pick with me, including at least one that had nothing to do with my failing to read that damn book.

He didn't like how I wrote for the Indianapolis Catholic newspaper, whose editor loved my column and ran it weekly. Unbeknownst to me, my teacher read me carefully and took this occasion my coming—to him under pressure, even threats, by the dean—to deconstruct my writing, characterizing it as inadequately respectful of data and representing in general an unseemly rush to judgment. He apparently thought it was time someone told me off, and he was the one, arrogating to himself this awesome responsibility.

As for me as student, which was properly his concern, I had been uncooperative, as in kissing off the reading assignment. He had me there. I had passively-aggressively challenged his authority and wounded him, which may be why he felt it necessary to go beyond his portfolio as teacher, negatively assessing my writing habits. I sat for it, having decided it couldn't be avoided if I were to survive the crisis. It was probably a bad tactic, however. I could have taken him up on any or all of it rather than just sat there. But I had written *him* off and was being purely pragmatic about it. Get past the crisis, I figured, and then regroup.

I ran into the dean a day or so later. He came out of his office to greet me. He was effusive: "Mr. Bowman, you're now a first-class citizen," he announced. I smelled b.s. but accepted his congratulations. All I had done was relieve the other guy of the burden of my ignoring him, and I was back in the saddle, a good theologian. Easy.

The dean's relief was palpable. He would not have enjoyed ousting me from theology. For him it was a happy, happy day. For me it was on to the next test of my willingness to toe the line. I was overdoing the line-toeing but did not know how to stop.

FERMENT IN SOUTHERN INDIANA

The course in question was in dogma. This was our term for doctrine, what the church had taught, was teaching, would never stop teaching. Dogma is a bad word in some circles, but it was a neutral one in ours. With the dogma course came an ingenious system of footnotes. Every statement of every church council and every papal pronouncement and anything else that had survived the winnowing process of tradition had a "note," or rating as to its reliability. If the statement was "de fide divina definita" (defined as revealed by God), it was a matter of faith: you could take it to the bank, and you'd better, if you wanted to call yourself a Catholic.

If it were anything less, down a ladder of assent, you had steadily decreasing certainty and obligation to endorse it. Notes were assigned by professional theologians, who did not always agree. They were learned by student theologians like us, who always agreed or were expected to. Some things were more certain than others. You could even have your own opinion about some, found at the ladder's bottom. The higher you went, the greater the risk of heresy for the denier.

This was systematic theology with a vengeance. It provided a framework for discussion and even a sort of mnemonic outline. It was belief calibrated. If it was in a way mechanical, it also imparted nuances that encouraged a sort of sophistication as to belief. The very notion of calibrating doctrine promotes a healthy relativism: not all doctrines are equal. This relativism, if you pardon the term, would stand the confessor, preacher, counsellor in good stead, and through him the faithful with whom he came in contact.

In fact, opinions could differ about a doctrine found on the lower rungs of certainty. Jesuits, more reluctant to assign the higher note, were known for being less restrictive. One teacher quoted someone as saying we Jesuits could be more liberal because we knew more. There was something in that to make a fellow sit up in the saddle.

In any case, theologians dealt in dogma, the church's arsenal of beliefs that had survived the centuries. We student theologians were to absorb them so that later we could defend and propagate them by what we taught and preached. My religion teacher at Fenwick would say, "If dogma won't do it [convince us to be good Catholics], nothing will." No one at West Baden cavilled at the word. This was the one, true church, and we its functionaries were to be schooled in its teachings.

My classmate Paul Quay, fresh from obtaining his physics doctorate, wanted us theologians (students) to be exposed to nothing but arguments against dogma in the first two months of theology. Shaken in our certainties, he figured, the more would we appreciate the faith once we had heard and given full study to the arguments. In that enterprise we would spend the rest of our four years. Deeply committed to the church, he wanted us exposed to doubt about it and God and everything else, so that we would keenly anticipate the answers we would get from our teachers and study.

You can imagine what a worrisome thing that would be, however. If the dean had a problem with me as recalcitrant student, what would he think of two months of faith-shaking? As intelligent and committed as Paul was, his was an idea whose time had not arrived.

Paul was a challenger of the accepted in other ways. Another theologian, a footballer from Cleveland and an incipient biologist who was to become a psychiatrist while remaining a Jesuit, took a walk now and then with the indomitable Quay. This was George

Murray, who would walk with Paul around the terrazo-floored atrium, head down, hearing Paul out.

Many made such walks during after-meal recreation, noon and night. We had grounds to walk on, but when weather forced us inside, we strolled under the world's largest unsupported dome, through whose overhead glass the sun shone in good weather, sometimes brightly. They made a noteworthy pair, Paul a gaunt fellow, George with a lineman's beefy solidity. George likened Paul's face, skin drawn tightly over high cheekbones, to the wind-tunnel look of a test pilot under G-force strain.

Joe Sikora was another walker from whom one picked up memorable commentary. He was a tall, somewhat stooped galoot from Chicago who had entered the novitiate with philosophy doctorate in hand and some very deep stuff in print or headed there—*Inquiry into Being* was one title. Catchy, I thought. The province fathers had unsurprisingly let him skip philosophy.

He caught up to us in a hurry and became part of what I found to be the rich conversational backdrop to theology. He once drew a helpful if elementary distinction between theology and church politics, something important to keep in mind in those years of Vatican Council 2, when the air was full of controversy. Joe was not about to be sucked in. He was a nice corrective to the whirlpools that swirled about us.

He served the same purpose when John F. Kennedy was shot, quietly cavilling at the community's absorption in it. I shared his feeling, noting something "ghoulish" about our spending so much time watching television in the auditorium, set up specially for the days immediately following the assassination. I was among those watching, in fact, when Jack Ruby, the Chicagoan with mob ties, shot Oswald on camera.

It had not been on television that I had heard of the Kennedy shooting, however. We do remember how we heard it, don't we? I can easily recall a first-year theologian walking down the hall knocking on doors, giving the awful news, "The president was shot."

Sikora also reminded me that JFK (and brother Bobby) had started investigation of steel executives who had raised prices, in the course of which the executives had been called at home by FBI agents. Most of us applauded JFK when he blew his nose. Even then there were very few Republicans among us. Sikora, on the other hand, was quietly critical, indeed appalled at those dark-of-night telephone calls.

Gene Kotz, a few years older than I, was a labor union specialist prone to support liberal causes but very data-based. He had a high-pitched voice and ready laugh. We had an elderly sociologist on faculty, Father John Coogan, whom he classed with neanderthals for his anti-union and other conservative stances. I never dealt with Coogan, but if I had, I would have heard from him something much like the positions I take today.

We had a ferment going. It was not as literary as I would have liked, but ideas were popping, largely about political and other current events. The place was lively in that respect. We supplied liveliness for each other. In addition, the writers among us got a boost when Maurie Moore, a Chicagoan, plugged us into the national Jesuit Writers Agency out of Weston, Mass. This met my needs and interests nicely.

TO WRITE, TO LIVE

I'd sold various pieces and kept up with writing stories, essays, and articles, especially once I returned to being a student. I did a weekly column for the Catholic newspaper in Indianapolis, as I mention above. I wrote stories, one of which won a Catholic Press Association award for best short fiction of the year for young people. It ran in Today Magazine in Chicago, one of the many publications I wrote for that are long since defunct.

The award was announced at table one night after the reader read the opening lines of my story, "Whiskey Cake," a slice of classroom life, and a letter saying that I'd won the award. The rector said the magic words "Deo Gratias," meaning we could talk. I hadn't seen that coming, my being the cause of Deo Gratias at dinner. A scholastic remembers things like that. I engaged in a flurry of writing in these years, selling a dozen or more pieces, fiction and other, to Catholic magazines.

In due time I got a book offer from Ave Maria Press, which wanted something on social issues as teachable in the classroom—a textbook or at least something usable by the Catholic school teacher who wanted to bring his charges up to speed on the day's hot issues. These were the early 60s, and the world was charged with rapid change, if not revolution.

I tried to write this book, joining the Indiana U.-bound contingent one Thursday, our weekly day off, to research the matter in the big library on its beautiful Bloomington campus. Plunging into journals, I found that Spanish-speaking immigrants were better employed and were making more money than Negroes (as we liberals called black people in those days), even though blacks had on average more years of schooling.

I took that smidgen of data, gleaned from a scholarly journal, as a sign of racial prejudice in hiring—a pretty simple equation that indicates the depth of my inquiry, which was not very deep. I'd have been better off working with fiction and literary essays to make my points. I was later to spend a full school year grappling with "social problems" in classrooms full of very skeptical senior boys. But no book came out of this.

I continued to plug away. Writing was something I had worked on and taken pride in since I was a kid—the writing if not the publication, which began in the juniorate, though I did have a letter in the Chicago Tribune as a Loyola U. freshman. If theology was painful because of the forced inactivity, it was also a benefit because it slowed me down and permitted creative juices to flow.

Here was my lifelong dilemma: write or die, but it was more fun to stay busy. Busy, busy, busy, and never a stray thought to be concerned with. Many the time I forgot my troubles once I entered the classroom as a teacher, either because of the good things that happened there—the class clicked along, students stayed busy, seemed to be learning—or the bad—disorder, a kid's wising off, my knowing I was not doing a good job. Either way, I found myself absorbed and up to a point pleasantly tired.

Teaching was good, and I missed it. But about writing there were two elements: one, that it had moments of satisfaction that nothing else provided, and two, I knew that if I didn't do it, I'd be missing out on what I seemed born to do.

THE CHANGING CHURCH

Meanwhile, there was another, worldwide, excitement surrounding the church itself—what came out of the Vatican Council, which pretty much coincided with my time in theology. The struggle was joined. I was rooting for the white-knight "progressives" over the antediluvian, neolithic conservatives. Cardinal Ottaviani and friends, opposed to the vernacular mass and all other things new and beautiful, were the bad guys. We had our information from the National Catholic Reporter and The New Yorker, where Xavier Rynne pseudonymously delivered detailed accounts.

Rynne turned out to be an East Coast canon lawyer, a Redemptorist, but at the time there was nothing to do but guess who he was. An insider, to be sure. Our Scripture prof, Joe DeVault, didn't know who he was, but he had friends over there—the Rome connection was never far away—who told him Rynne and the New Yorker had it right. Rynne provided a score card. We were an avid audience.

TEACHERS AND TEACHING

DeVault was a good guy, transparent and unthinking of self. He educated us in form criticism, on which we were weened as Scripture students. He was not dogmatic, but scholarly. I bought it a hundred per cent. This was literature, after all, the sort of thing I'd been waiting for. We even took a shot at Hebrew, and Hebrew terms, transliterated to English alphabet, were our daily fare. That said, he was, typically for one of us, primarily a scholar, secondarily a pastoral adviser. The mind is what mattered to us most.

The kindly Jim O'Connor, also transparent, so that we knew what we were getting, taught us canon law, lacing his treatment with samples of violations that hurt people caught in the ecclesial snare.

He educated us in the rights of Catholics, especially members of religious orders, especially nuns, who put themselves under the thumbs of sometimes unscrupulous people.

He spoke rapidly, much of the time in Latin, often leading up to a rule's exception, introduced by the Latin word for "unless," which was "nisi"—"knee-zee." His rapid-fire explanation, heavy on the glottal, would sound arguably like "walla-walla," repeated until at the end would come "nisi": "walla-walla-walla-walla knee-zee." He was thus known as "Walla Walla"—affectionately for the most part.

He prepared us for priestly ritual, as saying mass, then in Latin. We'd pair off and practice in one of many small mass chapels. O'Connor had to approve. At least one of our class, impatient with detail, had to go back and practice some more.

THE BRUISED REED

We also learned how to hear confession, not from O'Connor but in moral theology classes from Dick (Richard A.) McCormick. There was the ritual itself, "rubrics" to learn, as for all the sacraments— what to say and when. More important was how we dealt with the "penitent," the one who came to confess sins. Moral theology, or "moral," as we often called it, was about morality as dictated by "right reason" and by divine law as gathered and codified by church authorities.

We had procedures about what to ask the penitent, the better to lead him or her through the catalog of sins. You did such and such? How many times? Alone or with somebody? We did this because we were there to judge. In some rare cases, the sin may be "reserved" to the local bishop or higher, and we couldn't give absolution.

Otherwise, we judged the severity of the sin and prescribed penance accordingly—a certain number of Our Fathers (Lord's Prayer) or Hail Marys, sometimes a whole rosary, even all 15 decades.

We were to become qualified to judge in these matters after our two-year moral theology course. The two years culminated with our "ad audiendum" (confession-hearing) exam or exams. We had to pass our "ad auds," we would say (odd-owd). For the ad-aud we sat before a three-examiner panel, each of whom would take the penitent's role, confessing sins. It was up to us to deal wisely and responsibly with what we were told.

This was more than knowing mortal from venial sin and assigning penance accordingly, as delineated above. As confessors (the ones hearing confessions) we were also counsellors. As bad as the classification of sins sounds, our business was to save people, not condemn them. This theoretically might call for denying absolution, one's certificate of divine forgiveness. But the rarity of this is exemplified by the remark attributed in our circles to Cardinal Archbishop Medeiros of Boston in the middle of discussion with his priests of how to deal with people confessing birth control. "Deny absolution?" he said, horrified. "I would never deny absolution." Indeed, as I spelled out in my 1994 book, *Bending the Rules: What American Priests Tell American Catholics*, our bark was worse than our bite.

Preparing for ordination also meant getting used to the "breviary," an abbreviated version of the Divine Office, our daily obligatory prayer—Psalms, hymns, other Scripture passages, and single prayers that monks chant together in monastery chapels but other priests say (or said) on their own. Jesuits did no chanting. It was one of the key points of Ignatius Loyola's founding: Jesuits were absolved of the responsibility, which had been taken for granted by and for religious orders.

Even the itinerant friars, Franciscans and Dominicans, founded three centuries earlier, were expected to chant the office—from the Latin "officium," or duty—when at home in the priory; and of course the non-itinerant and much older Benedictines, Augustinians, and Carmelites had the duty in spades. Indeed, Father Martin Luther, the first Lutheran, chanted it as an Augustinian monk before becoming a Lutheran.

In any case, the daily private recitation, which could take an hour and was in Latin, was a serious obligation. As a kid, I had seen a visiting Jesuit leave our festive dinner table to say his office in another room. We took it for granted. It went with being a priest. As a Jesuit, I saw other priests saying the rosary instead, if a day was drawing to a close and the man was at the wheel of a car, for instance, unable to read the book. To miss it of your own fault, however, was something to go to hell for in those days, because you had shirked your sacred duty to do the church's praying. It was one of the things you were ordained for. The obligation came with being ordained deacon, the last "order" (of holy orders) before priesthood.

So it was that in the sacristy, the vestment-changing room, after our ordination as deacons—the day before ordination as priests—we got the word from Jim O'Connor, our overseer for ordination ceremonies, who greeted us in his dry, cartoonish manner: "Now you're ordained deacons, you can go and pray the mortal sin off your souls." By saying the office, that is. Black humor! Welcome to the serried ranks of God's chosen!

A PRIEST FOREVER

Ordination itself was festive indeed. One's family arrived for the big day. Unlike diocesan, or secular priests, who become deacons a year before priestly ordination, we did it with Jesuit efficiency, assembly-line-style—day one for subdeacon, day two for deacon, day three for priesthood.

My parents gave me a watch inscribed, "Jim from Mother and Dad, June 9, 1963." I bring it every few years to Kuba jewelers on Oak Park Avenue for a cleaning and resetting of springs. It's not worth it by monetary measurement. It's the only thing I keep for its sentimental value, though not solely for that reason. It's what I consult on the Lake Street "L" when a black guy asks me the time. It was given to me on what we thought was my day of days by my faithful and loving parents. Who wouldn't keep it?

I say day of days, but at 31 after 13 years a Jesuit, it did not have quite the punch as for the 24-year-old product of the Chicago archdiocesan system, for instance. For the Mundelein seminary graduate, ordination was the longed-for culmination of hopes born in the heart of the altar boy. We Jesuits, on the other hand, were first of all students and teachers and maybe scholars. At least one of my contemporaries left the society before ordination because he couldn't see being a hyphenated priest—priest-scientist, priest-astronomer, and the like—though the ranks of hyphenated-priest Jesuits stretch back to the beginnings.

For that matter, becoming a priest was not a clear decision for the founder. Ignatius gave the matter some thought. Results-oriented as he was, he chose to get ordained, because (my words) you ain't nothin' in the church if you're not a priest. Who would listen to you? How would you get the organization moving? How preach and baptize and bring the sacraments to foreign lands? How far would Francis Xavier have got in India without that cachet?

Being a priest, therefore, was what you did to advance the kingdom. It was a pragmatic decision. In 1963, as even in this day of scandal, there was nothing like a priest. People knelt at your feet, listened to you in church without raising a peep, told you their troubles and sins. It was a no-brainer that did not escape us newly ordained. We acquired duties that required respect, even from superiors.

When an overzealous, not to say aggressive, hospital chaplain pressed too hard for my mother's confession as she awaited surgery, I had no hesitation in telling him politely to bug off, such was the confidence I felt as an ordained of God. He had me by many years, but we were equally priests.

So the priesthood it was for us, even if we gloried not in the mysticism of it all. We also knew we were getting into something permanent. Dispensation from subdiaconate was rare, Jim O'Connor made quite clear, from diaconate "rarius" (very rare), from the priesthood "rarissime" (almost never). And while we were at it, dispensation from bishop's ordination, he would deliver with gusto, was "numquam" (never). No one could say, and I certainly never claimed it, that we did not know we were in for the long haul. Nor did we doubt the mortal sin business with the breviary, and off we went to pray the sin off our souls, whether we liked his black humor or not.

Not that ordination wasn't a festive day. Family showed up in strength, the dining room was filled with them for a great feast—with no reading at table, to be sure, nor silence except for grace before meal. I had my new watch, which I must have reported to the minister, who made no fuss, not even a grimace that I recall, such was the depth of my fall from excellence.

LOCAL BOY

Next day we had our first solo masses. Mine was at Our Lady of the Springs, the pretty little parish church in French Lick a mile or so away. Family was there for that, proud and happy. A few days later I ascended the main altar at the church of my boyhood, St. Catherine of Siena, in Oak Park; and with the help of two other priests, deacon and subdeacon for the occasion, celebrated solemn high mass. My picture was in the parish bulletin and in the weekly Oak Leaves. I was famous. And unbeknownst to me, my name was engraved on a corridor wall of my alma mater, Fenwick, a mile or so down the street, I discovered years later, when it no longer described my situation.

In the rectory before mass, I was told by one of the four assistant pastors that a "colored lad" was at the door to see me. It was a grown man, a onetime boxer, retired mailman and fellow writer whom I had met at a writer's workshop in the city a summer or two earlier, Harold Sampson. He was Catholic and had come for the mass and wanted to say hello beforehand.

The "colored lad" reference, made by the priest, a big handsome red-faced Irishman, without rancor, gives an idea of the insularity then plaguing the white community. Harold was an excellent man, nicely dressed, a South Sider whom it was my pleasure later to entertain at our house two blocks from this very rectory in the early 70s, when it was Winnie and me and babies made three, then four, then five (in that house). In a few years, therefore, my friendship with Harold spanned my transition yet to come from holy Jesuit priest to husband and father.

MY IOWA SUMMER

In June of 1963, however, a writing summer awaited me, at the State University of Iowa, as it was known, now just University of Iowa. I'd been accepted at the much acclaimed Writers' Workshop for the eight-week course in fiction, where novelist Vance Bourjaily was to be my teacher-supervisor. I couldn't get a room on campus at the Newman Center, but a local pastor was looking for a priest to take his place that summer while he visited his native Ireland. We corresponded—by U.S. mail, this being long before email and cheap long distance calls—and I got booked for my coming weeks in Iowa.

The town was Marengo, 30 miles on Route 6 from Iowa City and the university. Looking back, from a writing standpoint my living in Marengo was not a good idea: I could have gotten a dormitory room and plunged into life as a writing student, undistracted from my work of the moment. But the Marengo experience was a rich one for me as a priest and a chance to exploit my newly bestowed priestly position. Besides, it was broadening for me a city boy to live in a small town.

The priestly business began right away. On the plane to Cedar Rapids, my first flight, I heard a woman's confession. Young woman. Can't remember what it was about, wouldn't say so if I did. I do remember, however, her writing me at the Iowa parish where I had said I was going to live. She wanted to get together, which I took as overly keen interest in me rather than my pastoral style. There I was, bishop's oils barely dried on my consecrated hands, and some woman was making a play for me, I thought. The perils of announced celibacy! In any case, I did not respond.

Vance Bourjaily gave me encouragement enough, though he was clearly skeptical about where I would fit into the fiction landscape of the '60s. I know I felt like a square peg in round hole in the workshop, emphasis on "square." I wore clerics to class at first, taking it for granted that I would do so, but gave it up. A Catholic in the class of 10 or 15 students, a wheelchair-bound black guy whom I got to know, knew I took it for granted I'd wear them and knew also that most would object.

Bourjaily, a nice guy, encouraged me but also said I might consider a book of sermons. I heard him out with a straight face at his gentle enough putdown of my whole reason for being there, namely to get good enough to write fiction that would sell anywhere, not just in Catholic publications, which he also observed were "too easy" a sell. For me a priest, he meant, and for writers in general probably. Not so easy as all that, I found.

The Marengo parishioners, straight, honest people, provided the rich experience. Preaching to them on farmers organizing union-like at a time when National Farmers Organization was afoot in Iowa, I quoted the pope in support. This did not sit well with some. Here was my pattern: if the pope said it, I was supposed to say it too, even in matters too complicated for me to grasp, and for that matter maybe for the pope too. No matter where I went, I was one to use the pulpit to push a point of view, something I learned later as a pew-sitter to resent greatly.

In addition, ever ecumenical and interracial, I looked up the African Methodist Episcopal pastor in Iowa City, Rev. Fred Penny, calling then knocking on his door. He was five years into an illustrious career at his church, Bethel A.M.E., which had opened its doors in 1868. I got to know him and his family and invited them to Marengo, where parishioners put on a wonderful affair, full of food and fun.

There were six Penny kids in all, including two lovely daughters. Regarding them their father, an ebullient and friendly man, noted that he was leery of the attentions bestowed on them of a handsome black guy who had got acquainted with the family. "Guy like that can take a jump and leave a package," he told me. Rev. Penny died as pastor in 1994.

Meanwhile, the Marengo parish's housekeeper and I did not hit it off. She was a hausfrau in her 50s. I had no idea she expected to sit at table with me, as she did with the pastor. He and she were a comfortable pair, apparently; she and I were not. When my parents visited me there, she was most gracious with her meals, and I believe we put them up in the rectory, a white frame house on that small town street. Neither did I expect that.

It was only after I was back at Baden and corresponded with the pastor that I realized how put out she was with me. "Thank God she didn't leave," he wrote. It would have been an unmitigated disaster for him, whereas I would have welcomed the chance to fend for myself, after years of community life. As I said, I'd have been better off in a student dorm, with nothing but writing and student life to occupy me. Dealing with parishioners was broadening, but rectory life made for a doldrum experience. I was cordial to her as far as I recall, but she knew I found her no company, I'm sure.

SUPPLYING OUR SERVICES

Back at Baden, for the standard fourth year of theology we newly ordained were sent regularly on weekend "supply," as it was called, to parishes in driving or short train-ride distance. We went as far north as Indianapolis and Greencastle, a college town. We were strictly mass priests at Greencastle, where the pastor, an eccentric fellow who subscribed to *Gentleman's Quarterly*, reserved the preaching to himself and we were expected not to fraternize with the locals. The college was DePauw University. If its students came to this church for spiritual sustenance, they had to be satisfied with whatever Reverend Father came up with when he wasn't busy with *Gentleman's Quarterly*.

In other places we preached. It was where my heart was. One Sunday in a suburban Indianapolis parish I faced a full church with a state election coming up that included a referendum about right-to-work legislation. Naturally I was against it and considered my position divinely inspired and so preached in my usual pro-union vein. There I was, 31 years old, not having worked for money since I ran errands on Michigan Avenue for 75 cents an hour in the late '40s, spouting off to my captive audience on the basis of my reading papal encyclicals and having absorbed the wisdom of fellow theologian Gene Kotz. It was 1963, revolution was in the air, and by God I was part of it.

That was me from the pulpit: sock 'em bust 'em on social issues. A few years later, I gave a woman nightmares (an assistant pastor told me) at St. Denis parish on the white Chicago Southwest Side when I socked it home on the importance of allowing blacks into one's neighborhood. Earlier, I punched home the same message to a Rockford, Illinois, altar and rosary society. My heart was in the right place, but my technique needed tuning.

I even chided a Chicago-West Side black congregation just 70 blocks north of St. Denis—I'd go alternate Sundays to each parish, having a shot at whites and blacks—for being inadequately active in the revolution. I was gentle enough about it, but there I was, again never having held a steady job, instructing heads of families. It was a far cry from demanding correct punctuation from high school boys. But I'd had theology in the meantime and felt qualified. And I had my pulpit, did I not?

I also had entree supplied by the Roman collar. That plus an inclination not to think I knew it all, at least in person-to-person matters, was an asset. In Iowa, for instance, I found myself being on hand sympathetically and knowing when to say nothing in a domestic matter with a family whose husband and father had a habit of forgetting to wear his wedding ring. I swear, in some situations, the thing to do was just to be there. Even as the accidental priest I was as a Jesuit, that much was seeping through. It was something I came to value.

JOHN HARDON

Back to theology for the Jesuit fourth year, we were still students, weekend supply or not. One of us fourth-year theologians had put off his ordination or had it put off for him. He'd been on the edge of disapproval for some time for various reasons, but had told Father John Hardon, teacher of short-course classes and his advisor, that if they wanted him out of the society, they would have to carry him out. Hardon, who was to become a patron saint for conservatve Catholics, told me he approved of his attitude. Hardon also encouraged me in my writing. He himself wrote up one storm after another. There was always something in his typewriter. He was always publishing.

Some considered John Hardon simplistic and untutored in the ways of scholarship, and I can't say I ever was drawn to what he wrote. But he was a full-service human being, even if he did not recognize Mrs. Rossellini when she opened her door to him, a church-census-taking priest, in Rome, some years earlier, when he was a student. So what if she bore a striking resemblance to Ingrid Bergman? It cut no ice with Father John, who never went to movies. That's a story told of him, which if it ain't so, should have been. He had his idea of what mattered, and Bergman movies or any other kind didn't qualify.

It's funny how warm my memory is of Father Hardon. I never had him in class. We had little in common but being writers. But I recall talking to him in his room with pleasure. He had an ascetic, almost ghostly appearance but was anything but a cold fish. He clearly cared about people. Stubborn and intuitive about what constituted true religion, he became a hero to the recalcitrant right.

Another who had been delayed was ordained with us. This was Fred, who spent six years—probably a record—as a teaching scholastic rather than the usual three. It was a matter of finding a principal and rector who would recommend him. That's how it worked: you were promoted to the next level when approved by those responsible for you. It works that way in any well-run organization.

Not always well, it sometimes seemed. A novice of my time, a happy-go-lucky, friendly Chicagoan, desperate to be a Jesuit, was never admitted to vows. He could not make it past our novice master. He even appealed to Rome about it, but the society was not about to countermand the master, whose job it was to judge the matter. If it came to Father Master or Novice George, Father Master won every time.

CAUGHT BY FRED

Fred, on the other hand, had moved right along until it came to performing in the classroom. It was in his sixth year of teaching that he scored the coup that may have convinced superiors they could use someone like him. It was a case of Fred doing what he did a lot, thinking outside the box, helpful unless you do too much of it and people don't know what the hell you're talking about.

It was about a homecoming dance program, in which the sophomore class ad caught Fred's eye. He saw there what no one else had seen: the first letters of each line, reading down, spelled out a lubricious series of phrases that became the talk of the evening as word spread. This was nothing so obvious as "I call my girl friend Skippy [as in peanut butter] because she spreads so easy"—what a sophomore, later an attempted stand-up comic, wrote in an essay for me his teacher at Loyola Academy. This is the school, remember, from which Bill Murray was to graduate a decade later. Fun was in the air.

Fred may have heard about the lubricious message while prefecting the dance. No Jesuit looked so innocuous. He was the perfect spy. In any case, he heard about it and informed the principal, who informed the rector. A full-court-press investigation ensued. The perpetrators were discovered. They confessed. One was determined the evil genius behind it; he was expelled. The other suffered a rest-of-semester after-school jug, something to remember if he ever thought of doing such a thing again.

I had both in class. It might have been the class where I found a note awaiting me at my desk one day, quoting me from the previous day, when I had blown up at someone. "Shut up when you're talking to me," said the note, accurately reporting what I had said in my excitement, and one line below, the attribution—"Beev," for Beaver, as in "Leave it to. . ." the TV show to whose hero they thought I bore a close resemblance. Fun in the classroom.

Of the two homecoming-program perpetrators, the one merely punished was a swimmer who fit the North Suburban profile, which wasn't his fault; the other had a congenitally furtive look and was probably congenitally furtive. It was decided he did not fit in, I assume. I wasn't in on deliberations. In any case, Loyola was saving kids from the alleged rampant immorality of New Trier High School students—sex orgies on the beach and the like. New Trier, one of the nation's highest-achieving then and now, was our formidable public school competition for the minds and hearts of Wilmette, Winnetka, and the rest of the North Shore. It behooved us to offer a less orgy-prone alternative.

GRADUATION

I have digressed. Back in theology, student life continued. I was among the fourth-year fathers who one spring day challenged the rest of the theologate in softball. This was 12-inch with gloves, fast-pitch. In the course of the game, I speared a liner at third, reaching it at the absolute top of my leap. I can still feel it. Those sweet memories remain of what one did on the playing field, as I have said. Nobody else remembers it. I gain neither fame nor fortune from it. But I remember it with pleasure. There's something special about it. Keep that in mind next time you hear someone downgrade athletics.

The year ground to a halt. The "ad gradum" exam, or just "ad grad," came and went, the last of nine such oral exams with which we closed out a school year. They were in Latin, as I mentioned earlier—a half hour each for first and second years of juniorate and philosophy, an hour for third-year philosophy, the "de universa [philosophia]," or "day you," covering the previous three years.

Theology years one through three ended with hour-long exams. The ad grad (say "odd grahd") was two hours. It covered all of theology. The "gradum," in question was the "step" or grade to be achieved so that one might be solemnly professed, that is, could take "solemn," vs. simple, final vows. These were the usual vows of poverty, chastity (celibacy, not getting married), and obedience—each for the second time—and a special fourth vow of obedience to the pope.

I put "solemn" in quotes because I never could figure it out: either I was committed to poverty (living modestly and getting permissions), continent bachelorhood, and following orders, or I wasn't. Why solemn? Why final, for that matter, since we never took temporary vows? The answer is, they were the final seal of approval by the Society. You were still on probation, even after ordination. You could still be held up, you could still be expelled if you acted up.

The course was 15 years—the 15th I will get to. The solemn vow-taker took his vows not before 17 years. If you failed the ad grad or any end-of-year final before that, you qualified only for "simple" final vows, which by rights meant you were less committed to obeying the pope, though no one said that. More to the point, it meant you could never be provincial superior or rector of a major seminary.

Neither of those possibilities were in my playbook, but I was still pleasantly surprised, I should say astonished, to be told early in my 15th year of training, "tertianship," that I had passed my ad grad. Pete Fox had been giving long odds for several years on my passing my orals. It was pleasant to think I had somehow, against all odds, beaten them. I was misinformed, however.

I PASSED? NOT QUITE

The tertian instructor, a tall, gaunt New Englander of kindly manner and measured demeanor, gave me the word in his office early in the ten months of tertianship. However, it was a "clerical error," I learned 20 months or so later from John Connery, the provincial. I had completed a year of teaching as a priest at St. Ignatius and was running a summer enrichment program for neighborhood kids. In the mail had come word that I was scheduled for final vows in a few weeks—a year early if I had passed my ad grad as Father Instructor had said. I called Connery, who is better known in church circles as a major-league moral theologian (morality umpire) of the second half of the century. He said he'd get back. He did, with the clerical-error explanation. (Yes, Virginia, even Jesuits make mistakes.)

There I was busy with a summer program for which I had with

federal anti-poverty money set up my own office with telephone in a corner of the school building. It was 1966, we were "fighting poverty" the LBJ way. As someone who looked as if he knew what he was doing, I had looked very good to the folks downtown, who were deluged by highly questionable seekers after federal money for their various schemes and programs. But poverty money or not, I had a decision on my hands. I had to make the final plunge. The contented, wholly dedicated soul, full of the Ignatian "more" and dying to serve, would have rejoiced. I didn't.

Faced with a decision I hadn't seen coming, I blinked and called off the final vows. It was a signal to a number of people, including my mother, she told me later. All I knew was, it was time to put on the brakes. As for the ad grad, I had done well enough to earn the degree, if not solemn vows. This may have been standard. If you made it down to the wire, you got the consolation prize. I hadn't collapsed while questioned or denied the Trinity. I passed to that extent, and had my S.T.L.—licentiate in sacred theology—among my academic accomplishments.

But I have diverged from straight and narrow telling of my story, for which I make apologies. In any case, theology drew to a close. It was on to tertianship.

CHAPTER 6. BOOT CAMP II: TERTIANSHIP, 1964–1965

If at first you don't succeed, try, try again.
—U.S. Educator Thomas A. Palmer,
Teacher's Manual, 1840

Theology ended with a whimper. Tertianship was next, sometimes explained as third probation, after first week of novitiate (the first) and novitiate itself (the second). This was 10 months in relative seclusion, a la novitiate days, in a rural or far-suburban setting. Two other Chicagoans and I chose Pomfret, Connecticut, over Parma, a Cleveland suburb. We wanted to travel, I guess, though one of us had been in New England for several years, working incognito at an investment firm in Boston, the better to manage province funds in years to come. The Jesuits had many ventures going, educational and otherwise, and many members to take care of, as in sickness and old age. Much money was to be required. My tertian classmate had trained to be a reliable handler of that money.

We lived in one of those big buildings that fell into Jesuits' hands in the 30s, when depression undercut owners' ability to keep them up and live in them. It was St. Robert's Hall, named (by Jesuits) for Robert Bellarmine (1542–1621), one of the early Jesuits, an apologist and defender of the faith—a smart guy and a decent one too, who managed a degree of civility in the midst of acrimonious times, when wars of religion were being waged on battlefield and campus. And in publishing houses, where Bellarmine wielded a big pen.

St. Robert's Hall had its big house and grounds, including pool and tennis courts. I dove into not yet emptied pool one autumn day and found it bracing. Nothing was growing in it yet. The estate was fine indeed, with big trees and wide grassy spaces. But more attractive were the surrounding winding country roads where the walker could see for himself the kind of stone wall that Robert Frost said is unloved by something. He did not make his case with me. I loved those walls.

The walks were standard for us. If as an 80-year-old I do a lot of walking, it has much to do with what I did as a countryside-dwelling Jesuit. They put us outside the city in those days, in pursuit of seclusion. We found ourselves surrounded by nature, learning its joys. At Milford I'd stop while walking to see the red-winged blackbird swoop, for instance. In 1964 at Pomfret, 30 miles west of Providence, R.I., we had room to wander, as during the Long Retreat, our second 30-day run through the Spiritual Exercises. I know not what others found in this exercise, which I was practicing just 14 Octobers after my first, but I found it an endurance contest and nothing more.

AT SEA

For one thing, it was "dry" prayer time, as we called periods when in meditation nothing held the attention or, more to the point, fed a sense of well-being. I had neither "consolation," as we used the term, nor sense of verifying resolve. What had absorbed my attention at 18 at Milford under Bernie Wernert now escaped me. I'd skip meditations, just walking around the countryside trying to get my head together or at least stay calm. Ordained only 16 months, I was committed to the Jesuits and priesthood and was looking forward to my "apostolate," as we said then. But in general I was distracted and on edge.

My prayer life had pretty much evaporated. Later I told a shrink of my plight, and he registered astonishment, as if to wonder what I had going for myself if not that. I had no sense of where I was heading, except to heaven, I hoped, when I died. This I took for a bad sign.

Another scholastic, who entered the society a year after I did and had everything going for him—looks, *savoir faire*, social standing, a great smile, athletic and musical talent—said at one point with his million-dollar smile, that he couldn't wait to die. He left instead, well ahead of ordination, and later died.

"Do you want to be a utility infielder?" George Murray asked me in my room at Baden one day. The issue was focus. I remained (to a fault) open to possibilities. The world beckoned, but I stood like the philosopher's ass, unable to choose a path, starving to death.

Staying busy was important, but I had to stay busy building something. John Hardon made writing a top priority for me. Father Bill Mountain, giving the scholastics and me, not yet finally vowed, a three-day retreat at Ignatius, during the school year no less, made the same point, urging me to demand time off or somehow make time for writing. There had to be a way to beat this game. I was groping.

The kindly old tertian instructor and 30-day retreat master, a survivor of decades of goldfish-bowl life in the society, had adapted to his environment. But he was literate and fluent and intelligent and not overblown. He didn't take himself too seriously; I could take him seriously. If tertianship was a problem, he did not exacerbate it.

Neither did my two Chicago Province friends. One had trained at an investment house, as I noted. Working where he would not be recognized—considered important at the time—he had used a cover story. He was a man of consummate discretion and could pull it off. That was behind him, and he was now a tertian. He was unique among us in that he had some notion of finance.

We were shown a movie that in true movie-industry fashion mocked business and finance, in this case the Italian stock exchange. None of us gave a hoot about this, but in post-screening discussion, the once undercover Jesuit took vigorous exception to the depiction as inaccurate and scurrilous. He was a solid guy as to his Jesuit identity and a good companion for these months.

AVANT GARDE VS. PEW-SITTER CATHOLIC

Another tertian, not of the Chicago Province, later taught theology in Chicago. With him in due time, I had sharp disagreement that epitomized the learned theologian-pewsitting layman gap, stemming apparently from one of those wink-and-nod issues that never reach the pulpit.

It happened in the late 80s, when a colleague of his at Loyola, a layman in the philosophy department, was making waves with his claim that Jesus did not rise from the dead. My friend and I discussed it on the telephone, I in our kitchen in our house in Oak Park. Growing impatient with his fine points demonstrating uncertainty in the matter, I finally said, Look, either Jesus rose or he didn't. To which he unfortunately (and shockingly) responded that we should not "play the logic game." I couldn't take this, especially from a Jesuit, and our conversation ended abruptly.

My friend was thriving on a theology faculty, while I was doing the same as *paterfamilias*, and the twain were not meeting. My sophistication was not up to his. Question is, how common was such a twain-splitting among Catholics of the late 20th century? More common than is mentioned, it seems to me.

On the same topic, yet another Jesuit contemporary told me at a social gathering that it did not matter to him if Jesus had risen from the dead. This from a hard-working contributor to the Jesuits and the church. He did not want to play the logic game either, it appeared.

But neither would say that from the pulpit. It would have made a headline in the newspaper I worked on, I guarantee you.

ROXBURY

One of the more memorable New Englanders at St. Robert's Hall was the perceptive and funny Hugh Riley, a liturgy expert who'd studied in Germany. He was a species of Boston Irish that I appreciated. I got a pretty close look at the breed in my month's "probation" (within a probation) in a Roxbury parish. Roxbury was billed as black and slum, but compared to Chicago it looked pretty good to me, and I walked around it and got around the city in general, for instance taking the subway at night to attend a lecture at Boston U. by John Silber, who was to become its president. My wife and I were to visit BU many years later as father of a student, our Peter, for early visits. Later the the family came for his graduation—a lively affair in the heart of town.

My month in Roxbury, at St. John-St. Hugh parish, was a stimulating, welcome relief from rustic Pomfret, with all its stone-wall fences. My duties were churchly—mass-saying, preaching, hearing confessions, rectory-sitting on Sunday night when the four priests on staff went elsewhere. Not much else, as I recall, but I filled in gaps with my customary running about.

As I had done on the West Side at Ignatius, I moved around the neighborhood, zeroing in on the civil rights nodes, including a storefront on main-drag Bluehill Avenue. What the St. John-St. Hugh pastor, an assertive, outspoken type, didn't know about my meanderings wouldn't hurt him, I decided. But I chose to mention it at dinner, suggesting the use by these civil-righters of unused space at St. John-St. Hugh.

"Those people are communists," bellowed the pastor, a wiry, sharp-eyed man in his 50s, shouting me down. After that I kept my counsel. Hugh Riley followed me in the Roxbury probation, which he enjoyed immensely. But he reported back to me that the rectory staff considered me a communist and felt excluded from my comings and goings. I was secretive, in other words, and they were hurt, Riley reported genially. But you could have bowled me over with a goose quill by telling me they cared. In any case, I had pulled back defensively, writing them off, and they knew it.

Not all. One of them was unlike the rest. Not just in being black— this was Harry Furblur, the first black priest for the archdiocese— but in his being ordained just two years earlier than I and thinking like me. I could tell from his book shelf. He had books I wanted to read. Another of the staff, ordained just two years before Harry, had detective novels. Temperament and habit partly accounted for this, but also our seminary upbringing.

Two years made a huge difference in the early 60s. If you had (studied) theology during Vatican II, you became sharply aware of reform and revolution. Jesuit theology faculties were generally with the flow. At least they paid attention, some of the teachers avidly, though as is often the case, it didn't matter where they stood. So the likes of Harry Furblur and me had perked up and stocked up with new books and ideas, and that made a big difference. Years later we corresponded. He had left the priesthood and married, as had I. Nice guy, he was my friend in the rectory, though with his own work as assistant pastor he had hands full and did not accompany me in my rounds.

The parish housekeeper and cook lived in an upper floor of the rectory. One was young, good-looking, and of a manner called "saucy" in 18th-century novels. I was given a room near the stairway, and when the stairway light went on, as she was ascending for the night, I knew it. In fact, I think I had a switch in my room for the stairs. Hmmm. The mind and imagination raced. It was not the sort of thing you ran into in Jesuit houses. Nor in most rectories, I suppose.

The neighborhood, hardly a black ghetto, was such that nobody paid attention if you walked the streets in your cassock. I'd do so on my way to St. Hugh's for early-morning mass, walking from St. John's, where the rectory was. It had been a mostly Catholic neighborhood. Among the black newcomers were far fewer Catholics, of course. Habits were dying hard, however, and not just in what a priest wore on the street.

The city was the usual cauldron of interracial cookery. An Episcopal canon (monsignor, Catholics would say) was leading the charge for integration. His name was mud in the rectory, where the crusty pastor set the tone, as when he would yell out when a priest with a middle eastern name whom they all knew called, "Ask him if he's making any rugs these days." It was a sort of rough humor, but it showed who was ruling the roost. The Irish hadn't bit and clawed and cajoled their way up from greenhorn status for nothing. Of course the biting and clawing era was long gone.

So my education continued. (Was I a latter-day Henry Adams?) At least I was seeking it. Sitting in the rectory did not appeal to me, except when I was placed in charge of things on Sunday night and sat with my steak and bourbon in front of the TV set, happy as a clam. I was there to cover the phone, which never rang while I was there.

Just as well maybe, because of my funny way of speaking. I had reason on one occasion to call the police about something important, I forget what, and got a lesson in regional pronunciation. Identifying myself as Father Bowman at St. John's rectory, I was done in by my short "o," which came out a flat "a." Saint Jan's? The dispatcher asked, until I spelled it for him.

The funny-sounding Cincinnatian had told me in the first week of novitiate, "I like your accent." So in Boston. However, and this is odd, many times I sounded, even in Boston, like a New Englander. People told me that. Some said I sounded like a Kennedy. But I'd never been east of Ohio. It had to be the attention I'd given to my speech over the years of training, not just as to stuttering but also as to projection and pronunciation, opening my mouth wide, bringing the sound up from down deep, etc., per instruction by Willie F. Ryan at Milford and Jack Williams and Tony Peterman at Baden, all speech teachers, whose role in a Jesuit house of training was important and I think underestimated.

A MIDWESTERN LENT

In December, my Roxbury "probation" over, I resumed my highly restricted day-to-day life. In Lent, however, things looked up considerably. It was back to the home province for us non-New Englanders, sent off barnstorming throughout Chicago and Northern Ilinois. Pat Boyle and I drove out to Sterling to a high school where I talked up the Sacred Heart on the public address system. (Catholics of an age will remember the Sacred Heart.) Frank Bonnike, the principal, put me behind a mike in his office, and away I went, delivering the palaver. This was in the Rockford (Illinois) diocese, where Frank was a priest. He later married the sister of a grade and high school classmate of mine who had been a nun.

Also in the Rockford diocese, I gave a mission or retreat in the downtown parish, St. Peter's, which had a contingent of three or four priests on hand—with whom I had a good time. I held on to my habits of gadding about, however, and performed poorly in a scheduled talk for which I had not adequately prepared. An old priest at the dinner table made a remark that stayed with me. "Deus providebit," he said, using Latin for "God will provide," as in Genesis 22, "won't be enough." It was a neatly delivered mild rebuke from an elder.

A year or so later, in Chicago, I gave two eight-day retreats to nuns. Here I was the 34-year-old new priest in a chapel full of nuns, many of them more than twice my age. There were 70 in one group, 50 in another. The 70 were in south suburban Blue Island, where they comprised the entire complement of an Italian-origin community, each of whom before retiring for the night knelt and kissed the hand of the aged, revered mother superior sitting in the rear of the chapel.

One of these sisters I got to know, a woman of Polish ancestry about my age. Race issues were to the fore. She told of one of their sisters who had been surprised by a black man in a sacristy. Did he touch her? I asked. "Touch her? He plowed into her!"

The other eight-day was for 50 BVM sisters at Immaculata High School on Marine Drive, near the lake. I made it up as I went along, scrambling to pull together notes, scribbling or typing conferences with minutes to spare, brazening it out.

Bad habits here, but I discovered I could do this and was willing to do it. I tried to deal with emerging issues, for one thing. My leanings were for what I considered reform, of course, but I tried to gain a sense of what was going over and what wasn't. I would chat with someone who told me what I was doing, and this way I could make changes more or less on the spot. Some objected—one nun grimly in my room to my face—to my not following the Ignatian

Exercises such as she was used to. Not all welcomed the ferment, nor do I blame them. Again, there I was, newly hatched as a guide for perplexed souls, telling veterans how to lead their lives.

A Jesuit who had entered Milford with me—a day earlier because he'd gotten a ride down there from his native Gary, Indiana—drew the line at dealing with the new nuns. They wanted group discussions, for instance; and Joe, a solid citizen and math teacher of normally patient disposition, wanted none of it. He too left the society and married and taught math as a layman, disappearing from the sight of us former colleagues.

He was one who left, I recall, not to protest anything or not mainly to marry, but because the new church was nowhere he wanted to be as a priest. Another said as much in an announcement letter: he was leaving because the priesthood wasn't what it used to be. Support was missing that used to be there in a more tightly knit Catholic community. I can't say I felt that. The support was there for the kind of Catholicism I was promoting.

CONNECTICUT CLOSING

Meanwhile, returning to tertianship, our Lenten preaching completed, we returned to St. Robert's Hall for our final months. We did supply from there too, of course, going on weekends to say mass, preach, hear confessions. I went several times to a boys' prep boarding school in Connecticut, where giving a retreat to the boys, I declared what to me was a no-brainer, in answer to a question, I believe, that fornication was a mortal sin.

One young man, surprised at that, seemed shaken. But a few weeks later, he seemed anything but. I met him on another visit to the school and concluded from his demeanor that he had seen through my position or thought he had. I had entered briefly the world of Joyce's Stephen Daedalus—not as Stephen Daedalus but as one of his Jesuit teachers.

An admirable young couple ran the school, which was in a summer-camp-like setting in rural Connecticut. They had many small children, whom you could not miss around the place. The two parents were tall, good-looking, healthy, and committed to the church's anti-birth control position, or at least did not feel free to ignore it. Chatting with them once, sitting in deck chairs on the grounds, I got the sort of look at married life that a priest could pick up. Sex in marriage, said the man, with whom the wife was in evident agreement, was for him "just somewhere to put the seed." And they appeared by no means pitiful people, just realistic about the life they had chosen.

There were other things to learn about being a husband and father. One of the teachers, deciding if a certain musical group was to perform for the boys, said in my presence that he disapproved of the group. I asked him why, being of a liberal bent and favoring permission in general over prohibition. He just didn't like them, he said, implying that their performance would work harm on the boys. I nodded without entirely getting it.

But in time I realized he was on to something. Long before Tipper Gore went after seamy lyrics as the vice president's wife, there were people like this teacher who objected to things that I in my pre-parental, liberal-Jesuit ways did not. I had read and studied more than he, but he had better instincts.

CHAPTER 7. PRIEST AT LARGE: CHICAGO AND CINCINNATI, 1965–1967

The priesthood is a very fulfilling life. But it's not an
ego trip. There are sacrifices in this life.
          —Fr. James Cassidy, Ecumenical Officer,
          Diocese of Northampton, U.K.

Leaving tertianship, I asked to spend the summer at a writers' house in Evanston, Canisius House, a block or so from the lake. The man in charge was John Amberg, who headed Loyola U. Press. He welcomed me, hanging my picture on the wall with other writers.

Such a deal it was. I had nothing to do but write. During the previous summer, at the U. of Iowa writers workshop, I'd got a fair amount of fiction written and a "B" from my teacher, novelist Vance Bourjaily. I had a novel to write. But having nothing else to do was not a good formula for me. I found myself lolling on the beach a few steps away and otherwise hanging about. Jack Trahey, a year behind me in the course, was living there as a doctoral student at Northwestern U. in drama. Otherwise, I was in Endsville, with all respect to the five or six older Jesuits who also lived there.

So in a few weeks I was off to Ignatius, where I was to teach in the fall, and my picture was off the wall at Canisius House. It was an omen. In my remaining three years in the Society, I was to move three times.

SUMMER AT ST. IGNATIUS

At Ignatius I settled down to some writing, not of the novel but journalism. A summer enrichment program was in full sway at the school. Jack Arnold and other scholastics had organized a program for neighborhood boys who otherwise would never darken the school's doors. I tagged along with them and wrote that up. It became a cover story later in a national Catholic magazine. Ditto for one I wrote on the summer's civil rights agitation.

For the latter I tagged along with a Newsweek intern whom bureau chief Hal Bruno introduced me to. I'd got to know Bruno through my brother Paul, who headed the Chicago ad office. Bruno thought a lot of Paul, noting for instance how he treated the black shoeshine boy who came up to the office. Some gave him a hard time, picking on him for laughs, but not Paul, who treated the guy well.

Bruno was a good guy. It was fun sitting in his office talking about the job he was doing. They had done a major story on crime in the cities but had to wait for a cover picture showing a white criminal. It took a while, and the story was put on hold. Bruno did not sympathize with this 1965 correctness, but the news industry was already minding its p's and q's in that matter. Dishonesty was replacing hostility to blacks—then still "colored" or "Negroes," of course.

He had two interns that summer. One was sluffing off his responsibility to learn the city. He was good enough to do what was asked of him—write reports for filing to New York. But he wouldn't read up on Chicago. The other did. It was with him that I attended a rally in a Winnetka park where Studs Terkel was m.c. and spoke of "waiting for Godot" with reference to waiting for the main speaker, Martin Luther King, who was late.

I ran into Ed Rooney of the Daily News on this occasion. He was friendly but noted that I was not marching or protesting but writing about it, this with a glimmer of criticism, as if a real priest marched. All in all, it was a great time. I wandered around with notepad doing what reporters do. I loved it.

FULL-TIME TEACHING

But the time came, in the fall, to go to work full time. I had discussed this with my old teacher, Bob Harvanek, who was province director of studies, going over possibilities with him as to my employment after tertianship. I had my "teaching master's" in English—no thesis, two extra courses—which meant I qualified as a high school teacher.

I hesitated. But Harv told me that in the last ten years only three priests had gone from tertianship directly to teaching in a high school in the Chicago Province, which had four high schools. In other words, the thriving high school network was understaffed as to young priests, which was a measure of the foolishness then abroad among us. There we were with this proven "apostolate," as we used the term, our high school work, and greener pastures were beckoning our younger men. I was shocked at that and decided I should go back to high school. How strange that I would have hesitated: when I'd started theology, all I'd wanted was to do just that. Back to Ignatius I would go.

Come September, I was back in the classroom, teaching "religion-slash-social problems" to seniors. It wasn't my idea, though in view of my interest in social problems, I was a natural for it. Rather, the principal, a few years my senior in the Society, assigned me to it, though without any instructions that I recall. Not that I was looking for any. Each section met three days a week. Another young priest taught the marriage course, also for three days. We each had our sections for a semester, three sections each. So by year's end, each had taught six out of seven seniors. The prolific textbook author Mark Link had the 4-A seniors.

BLACK AND WHITE

I jumped in with both feet, tackling race relations as our first social problem and assigning a 1964 book, *Crisis in Black and White*, by Charles Silberman. There was no point in being abstract about it, I figured, though even abstractions set my white students' teeth on edge. For instance, I also assigned a pastoral letter from the U.S. bishops on racial justice which got them even more upset than Silberman.

I had one or two black students per class. In at least one class, I had none. One of the blacks, son of Chicago public school administrators, was a basketballer, a big, good-looking guy, easy-going and his own man, and actually a student fans' favorite. He told me once that there were guys in his section who would do him in if they ever got him in a dark alley, however. He was quite Chicago in his understanding of how things work. He also took a good-looking white girl to the senior prom, sure of himself as ever.

When I took him down the street to meet the local organizer-agitators at the West Side Organization, I was treated by them as God's gift. One of them, known as a tough guy and an ex-con shook my hand warmly. I had delivered a sort of Barack Obama and was justifying the school's presence in the neighborhood. The young man never went back, however, as far as I know. He was too shrewd to be drawn in by the Roosevelt Road con men, ex-con or otherwise.

Another black student, a son and nephew of Pullman car porters, told me at the start of the term that he would be watching me closely as to how I handled black issues, which was nervy of him. I did not think so at the time, however, and took it as a challenge. Of special concern to him was that I might name successful blacks only in sports and entertainment.

On another occasion, not related to this caveat but still serving to relieve me of stereotypical notions, he noted that his family would drive many blocks into white neighborhoods to get the kind of pastry they liked. He later joined the mostly white junior Catholic Interracial Council, a dozen or so kids for whom I became a sort of chaplain. Much later he wrote for Muhammad Speaks, the black Muslim newspaper—without becoming a Muslim. And he informed me when I ran into him years later on an "L" platform, that the military draft was a "paper tiger" which he had avoided easily.

MRS. DALEY REACTS

In the first class meeting for one of my sections, after I announced that we'd be reading *Crisis* and talking about race, one of the students, Bill Daley, the mayor's youngest son, came up and asked where I'd grown up. I said "in the Austin & Madison area." I didn't say Oak Park, which would have been only half right anyway, because Chicago's Austin was part of our neighborhood, but neither did I want to locate myself in suburbia. He had read the book that summer, I learned later. So had his mother, or at least she knew about its part that told of their Bridgeport neighborhood rising to expel blacks who unwisely moved in there.

The book was "nothing but newspaper stories," she told the principal later in one of her irate phone calls that gave him stomach aches in the coming weeks. "Are they?" he asked me. I told him no, but even then, years before I had joined the newspaper business, I saw no condemnation in that if it were true. I trusted newspapers.

Running out of things to say to my restless students, I got a small budget for speakers. One of them, a black guy from the Mayor's office, was given a hard time by students. Bill Daley, defensive, complained to me in a written report on the session for not interfering. I wrote back in essence that it had been a judgment call, that generally I tried not to interfere with discussion.

Another speaker, a young black guy experienced in teaching Catholic high school boys, was far better at engaging the students. He sent me out of the classroom for his talk, which ended with Bill and him yelling at each other, I heard from other students. The guy was dynamic and knew what he was doing, however. Months later, when I had him back for another appearance, I saw him and Bill talking after class in friendly fashion. But the guy apparently used "hell" or "damn" or both in my classroom, and that gave Mrs. D. her opening for yet another stomach-churning complaint to the principal. The rector, Bob Koch, who was very patient with me amid all this, told me about her complaints, but never with so much as an admonition.

A MAYORAL CONFERENCE

Mid-term came around, and time for parent-teacher conferences. Bob Koch asked if I'd be willing to meet the mayor separately. The mayor and his Mrs. had waited their turn in previous years for such conferences, but this time the discussion would get tense, and so privacy was in order. I said fine.

There was an element here of not bucking City Hall, what with the school being in an urban renewal area where land was being given or sold cheap to worthy institutions. What's more, the school was somewhat on the bubble financially, or very much on the bubble—I was not on the inside of such matters—and I felt responsible.

So I called up City Hall and left my name and number. That night the Mrs. called from the Lowe Avenue home. I said that with the mayor being so busy and all, maybe he and she could come (with Bill) to their conference at some time of their choosing. "Just a minute," she said, then came back on. "We'll be there in fifteen minutes," she said.

I greeted the three, plus driver, who waited outside the parlor, at the Roosevelt Road front door. We went into the nearby parlor, across from the elevator. For the next half hour, the city might have been sliding into Lake Michigan, for all the mayor seemed to care. I had his whole attention, and needless to say, he had mine.

I opened with "I think I know why you're upset," but the Daleys were having none of it. "You're the one who called the meeting!" said Richard J. Oh. No niceties here: these parents were pissed, I was the enemy of the hour.

Bill had done poorly in some tests, I told them. "What tests?" asked the mayor. Oh. It was challenge time. I excused myself and took the elevator up to my 4th-floor garret, retrieved the tests, and brought them down and showed them.

One was about the California labor organizer Cesar Chavez and the braceros, from an article in *America* magazine. Both were standard reference points in the circles I was reading in and touch points in a social problems/religion course.

"What's a bracero?" the mayor asked. I told him—a migrant worker in California. Not good enough. He spoke in flat tones, only his mouth moving. None of my explanations satisfied him as we went through other subject matter of the course.

He was out to discredit me, I realized, before the son, who sat saying nothing. It was standard for the son to accompany parents to conferences. I don't recall being surprised to see him—this in contrast to the dozens, I am tempted to say hundreds, of teacher conferences my wife and I attended for our six kids over 27 years in grade, junior high, and high school, when the son or daughter did not come along.

Neither did Mrs. Daley say anything. She certainly was not embarrassed, as my mother would have been if my father were pressing an issue with some heat. She was wholly in his corner. The mayor spoke for both.

He had one substantive objection. "What does this have to do with religion?" He said it was unlike any religion teaching he had ever heard of. I believed him. So there I was, no good at the half measure and having pretty much decided that social justice was the be-all and end-all of religious practice, and I had the mayor of Chicago challenging the notion. Not bad, when you get down to it, for witnessing to one's belief in a high place.

Not that I made the most of the opportunity. I had no stomach for an argument and gave the soft answer. At one point my gorge rose and I was about to respond in kind. But this would not have done the school any good. Besides, I was presumably trying to be Christian about it, and so I let the gorge deflate.

The mayor turned to Bill at one point, admonishing him to work hard or something like it. And another time, maybe three-quarters through, he said something construable as compliment, "Well, you believe in what you're teaching," he said, conceding to me briefly the courage of my convictions. This remains with me as inexplicable in view of his general instransigence.

MIKE ROYKO GETS THE STORY

One of our disagreements was with what I'd written on something Bill had handed in. He had waxed eloquent with his point of view when the assignment had been to report what had been said or written—a sort of exercise in objectivity. Viewpoints were what we traded in class, which in Bill's case was all white. I set up certain rules for our discussions, as never to say "nigger." Opinions flew hot and heavy. But in some writing assignments, I ruled them out. "Give me what the man said, not what you think," I had written on Bill's paper.

The mayor missed my point or chose to ignore it; and as they left, he turned to shake hands, and in a burst of sarcasm said, "I'll tell him [Bill] he's to give you back just what's in the book!" Then they were gone, the driver holding the door open.

Adrenalin pumping, I left the building by the back door and headed into the yard for some walking around. Next day I filled Bob Koch in on it. He didn't say much, but I think he appreciated my holding back and in general putting up with the situation as it developed.

A few years later, I told Mike Royko about the whole business, and he put it in *Boss*, his book about Daley, in the part about Daley's attitudes towards blacks. Mrs. Daley tried to get a Bridgeport supermarket not to stock it, which Royko duly publicized in his column. But a few years after that, doing a story about Ignatius, I talked to a student carrying his paperback copy of *Boss*, which he was reading as a class assignment.

Bill and most of his classmates, realizing I meant business with my assignments, did all right the rest of the semester. There were no more meetings with the Daleys. But at year's end, when I was up on the altar with other priests at a baccalaureate mass, the mayor came down the aisle for communion, our eyes met, and in his was no benevolence. I had crossed him, and he hadn't forgot. Years later, Royko wrote in the copy of *Boss* he autographed for me, "He knows it was you [who told about the parlor conference]. Beware!"

JESUITS REACT

Meanwhile, before the year was out, 1965–66, I had done my best to swing my white students around. The only sign I had that I did so was the comment in a semester-end paper by one of them that before the class he had joined others of his neighborhood in driving into nearby black neighborhoods to find a black and beat him up. Now he wouldn't be doing that any more.

From my colleagues I got various reactions, mostly along lines of age. A Jesuit religion teacher who emphasized the inner life for his students, vs. my emphasis on behavior, told me he was doing more for the race problem than I was. I did not argue with him, at a loss as to how either of us would know. A lay teacher whom I knew better than most from his years in the Jesuits, cut me off one day as an extremist for some position I had taken in class. I had gotten defensive, at that, falling into the old loss-of-perspective trap, as in not conceding that there was no justification for the black kid flashing a knife at whites on an "L" train, for which indeed there was none.

The principal was in general not happy with how things went, on one occasion demonstrating his disapproval in another context by breaking into my classroom one afternoon—while I was there—to tell my students to be quiet. The door to the classroom, down the hall from his office, was open, and I was reading from *Catcher in the Rye* for a once-weekly Creative Writing class, and the boys were roaring.

COMPANY MAN • 189

The students reacted well, reading the interference as uncalled for. I told Bob Koch about it. I considered him on my side, or at least sympathetic with my position. He was certainly one I could level with, even when he boiled over at me, as he did once. I was eating my steak in the two-story fourth-and-fifth-floor grand library turned rec room on a feast day. My various neighborhood activities were in his craw, and he crossed the room, which was full of Jesuits, to upbraid me, I forget about what in particular. But he was a straight guy whom I could put off in relaxed fashion with "Now's not the time I want to argue about that, Bob," at which he went back to his steak. This was an aberration.

We had barbecued on the fire escape, by the way, a stone's throw from the projects. It was probably July 31, St. Ignatius Day, and all in all, the kind of nice experience, sitting and chewing the fat with the brethren, that endured as a nice memory, even with the rector pissed off at me. He wasn't someone I could hold a grudge against anyhow. In fact, I'd have to class him with Mike English of Loyola Academy and John McGrail of the juniorate and Bob Harvanek of West Baden as men I had as superiors or teachers whom it is a pleasure to remember after these many years—each a man in whom bullshit had no place.

As the 1965–66 academic year had wound to a close, a lay teacher whom I had known when he was a student in my year at Ignatius as a scholastic in 1957–58, thought I should ask out of the whole religion-social problems business and teach English. It was not a bad idea, not least because the content of religion-social problems was nonexistent. In how many ways was I to urge my students to do right? After a while at it, I would be reduced to spitting out data that made my point.

Decades later, it occurred to me that I'd have been better off teaching the course out of literature, assigning novels, essays, and even poetry for its combination of rhetoric and insight. On the other hand, at a 50th-anniversary reunion of the Loyola class I taught in the '50s, I heard from one of them that our field trips to the black South Side were life-changers. In any case, I chose another route out of my situation, unfortunately. I went back to school.

This made no sense. Caught up in an imaginary power game—wanting power so I could "make a difference"—I decided I should be a sociologist, because "knowledge is power." What I was doing planning how much power I could gain—to do lots of good, of course—is one of the mysteries of the '60s. I had joined as an 18-year-old as if coming home to a divine certainty. Sixteen years later, a thoroughgoing creature of my time, I was just another influence-seeker—to do lots of good, of course.

My first year as a priest-teacher had gone well, all things considered. I had people mad at me, including the principal, but there was nothing terminal about that. In fact, years later he and I met at a reunion and shook hands and were glad to see each other. So people were mad at me. It was nothing I couldn't handle. Nothing others couldn't handle either, as far as I could see. The student newspaper played me up as Ignatian of the Year or something like it, in honor apparently of my having made a splash.

SCHOOL AGAIN

But I had great things on my mind, not realizing I had great things already in hand. Off I went next door, to the U. of Illinois campus, when I should have just held my ground and taken the next year's assignment. But in a combination of impatience and sense of vocation within a vocation, I got myself declared a student.

I probably could have used some counseling in the matter—something on the order of Bob Harvanek's telling me how few newly ordained had gone into high school work. One guy, not a superior, tried – Bill Mountain, mentioned earlier, a serious, friendly, quietly straight-talking fellow, who had put it to me during the three-day retreat at Ignatius, in my year after tertianship. Bill's was the right idea, to drop everything and just write. But if I couldn't put in a summer writing at Canisius House, how could I do it full-time?

I lasted a semester at U. of I. It was a pleasant enough experience. My marks were O.K. The people I dealt with—my advisor Bob Corley, teachers, and fellow students—were decent and personable. One student, in his 30s like me, had done time for manslaughter, which I saw he might have achieved with his ham-sized bare hands. Fallen away from his cradle Catholicism, he said he wouldn't have fallen away if he'd known a priest like me. (Maybe.) Corley, a veteran sociology prof who was later a dean, commandeered me on one occasion for proctoring an exam; this gave me practice in using my eagle eye to spot cribbing. It was all in all a pleasant time.

FREE-LANCING

But after one term, the fall quarter, I bailed out. Again, no questions were asked by superiors that I recall. They may well have been acting with great care with young Jesuits in that time of flux. I was getting my way, remaining the genial talented fellow I had always been, floating along. How talented came to me with a shock when applying for the U. of I. program and among documents requested came a report of my IQ score when entering high school. It was a shock because it was very high and I felt I had little to show for it. To whom much is given, etc. Something was wrong.

It was known in the province that I was loose again when I visited friends at Loyola Academy during Christmas break. I ran into Mike

English, who asked if I had a minute. We went into a nearby visitor's parlor. He said he had a high-profile priest teacher who, "nervous from the service," was leaving the Jesuits. Mike was straight about it as usual: If I took his place as a religion teacher, I could help people forget him and show that there were more in the Society where he came from. It was a good offer, which I took seriously. I took a few days to think about it and called Mike back on New Year's Day, first wishing him a happy new year and then saying I declined.

The provincial's office found work for me to do. I gave a retreat in Barrington, another in Milford, both at the men's retreat houses. I gave retreats also to nuns, mentioned earlier as exercises in *chutzpah*. I did this and that, filling in and staying busy. And of course, I roved the neighborhood, having appointed myself ambassador to the projects. I went knocking on doors across the street in the high-rise. I walked down Roosevelt and into the low-rise buildings that were also part of ABLA "homes"—Abbott, Brooks, Loomis, Addams— getting to know people, becoming a familiar face.

THE STREET

Down Roosevelt a few blocks, past the projects to the west, was the storefront headquarters of the West Side Organization, more or less headed by an ex-con named Chester Robinson and funded in part, probably large part, by the Union Church of Hinsdale. Yes, upscale suburban Hinsdale. Rev. Bob Strom, the quintessential white liberal Protestant activist who brought Union Church into the civil rights revolution, was the connection. Friendly, good-looking, the size of a linebacker, he had his apostolate, as it were, among the black downtrodden. The WSO storefront office hosted meetings and other gatherings. I was welcome as a useful idiot if nothing else. It became one of my ports of call.

I was on or near the cutting edge. It's what the activist priest did. I was engaged, relevant, and open-minded. Apart from all that, I was getting an education in what was going on in American cities. I'd sit in a meeting at WSO while Robinson cracked wise about how the white people who came around were smiling all the time or ogled black women. I listened to the angry rhetoric. I came calling at night after riots and found Chester, Rev. Strom, and friends partying with food I had cadged for the needy from the Ignatius kitchen—and smoking something pungent while they were at it. Very interesting, all of it, contributory to my ongoing inoculation to the appeal of the civil rights professional.

THE BOARD ROOM

In those days I was also on the board of the Interreligious Council on Urban Affairs (IRCUA), where Msgr. Jack Egan was the Catholic linchpin-figure and co-organizer. He and his friend Rev. Edgar Chandler, of the Church Federation of Greater Chicago, had started it with the help of a rabbi who had dropped out by the time I showed up. His place was taken by Rabbi Robert Marx, who filled out the American triumvirate delineated by Will Herberg in 1955— Protestant, Catholic, and Jew.

We met downtown, at the Church Federation offices on Michigan Avenue. We were presumed urban-problems specialists from then-mainstream denominations. Among us was a distinguished geographer from U. of Chicago named Harold M. Mayer, a paunchy, dumpy-looking man in his early 50s, who shook his head as the "race problem" was discussed as solvable, indicating that he saw no solution. But he was one voice. For the most part, hope was springing.

Lew Kreinberg was there for the Jewish Council on Urban Affairs. He worked in Lawndale with Father Dan Mallette, pastor of St. Agatha parish, and other mostly young priests and citizens. Lew's wife had their child at Cook County hospital, of which I was informed by Tom Gaudette, a Catholic-parish-based community organizer in the Saul Alinsky mode who lived in Beverly. They were two different kinds of radical.

Gaudette had no use for what he considered the aimless, hands-on, theoretical-leftist Kreinberg approach. He reported this baby-delivery item to me as reflecting badly on Kreinberg, who had grown up in (also upscale) Highland Park. Kreinberg apparently took it in stride, being of the people as he saw it and committed to breaking from the middle-class mode. Gaudette, on the other hand, parish- and institution-oriented in his work, saw no benefit to anyone in living like the people he wanted to help.

THE MONSIGNOR

Jack Egan had recruited me for the IRCUA. I had met him in one of my early-'60s summers in Chicago while a theologian. My classmate Pat Henry and I, the two of us working at settlement houses between years of theology, had gone to meet him at his office on Superior Street near the cathedral. It was in a converted three-story stone front residence with big windows looking out on Superior. Jack saw us after his nap; he was taking one daily since his heart attack, suffered months earlier while with Edgar Chandler, who had called for help.

In his office at one point with Pat and me, he stood looking out of the big window while enunciating somewhat melodramatically his vision for the city. Pat and I looked at each other. We weren't used to such a display. Years later, after Jack had made one of his sweeping forays into the city room, Royko came over to my desk.

Impressed, he likened Egan to the Bing Crosby priest-character in "Going My Way."

So he was, if you add a touch of irascibility that popped up now and then. Winnie and I went to his 40th-anniversary ordination celebration at a beer hall near Cermak Road, Sauer's, as did the Callahans and Sullivans, Oak Park couples, with whom we gathered afterwards.

Gene Callahan had been executive director of the Chicago Conference on Religion and Race, formed after a 1963 gathering, and later was an Oak Park village trustee. He had been close to Egan and had named one of his sons after him. But they had drifted apart at the time of this 40th anniversary, in 1973. Gene went anyhow and afterwards marvelled at how resentment melted away at the welcome he got from Egan. It was difficult to remain at odds with him.

Later, Jack put in a word for me at the Daily News and probably had more than anyone else to do with my getting my job there. But in the '65–'67 period, he was part of my wandering from what I now consider would have been a more reliable path. He wanted me on his side, and I profited in a number of ways from joining his team, but my best bet would have been to go Jesuit in all I did, clinging to everything Jesuit and tending to my spiritual life. Or so it seems 45 years later.

ASKING PERMISSION

Not that I went off on my own. I tested my initiatives, as it were, putting my ideas to various superiors along the way. In the summer of '66, for instance, I drove down to Mississippi to march with James Meredith, who had been shot while marching but had recovered. The provincial, John Connery, gave the go-ahead, remarking in his laid-back fashion that I was riding a hobby horse.

But in no way was I harrassed for it or other out-of-the-way ventures. My classmate Pat Boyle said something to the effect that I'd make a good point man for the province in these matters, because I could be counted on not to do something stupid. Another Jesuit said much the same thing.

Indeed, as an activist priest, I was fairly conservative, doing my best to dot i's and cross t's. I took a day to decide to go to Mississippi, for one thing, astonishing a young nominally Lutheran hotshot who worked with us on organizing high-rise residents. This fellow, full of misguided enthusiasm, told a young black man he shouldn't trust whites, for instance, he himself being white. His was an impulse-driven approach. Mine wasn't.

Once I was in Mississippi, I spent half the day on pay phones trying to get the local bishop's permission to say mass at roadside. When the bishop nixed it, I went looking for the local priest nearest the marchers' camp for a place to say mass. The local man, a foreign-born Irishman ("FBI priest," we called such, who were more prevalent in the Protestant South and rural areas than elsewhere), gave me access to his little church for mass.

I visited him in his rectory in the white part of the small town where I was to spend the night, rather than at the camping grounds, where most stayed. The black man who was putting me up drove me to his house and waited outside. The priest and I had a good long talk, 45 minutes or so. He was not in favor of what I was doing and tried to talk me out of it, alleging publicity-seeking as my motive. It was for a good cause, I said. But our conversation was not acrimonious.

My black driver did not wait in the priest's driveway—partly, I figured, because he did not relish being asked what the heck he was doing there. The priest drove me back to the black part of town, to a general store which offered "sundries," where I reunited with the family whose house I was to stay in. I got into a car that took me to a neat, comfortable house and was shown my room with its clean and comfortable bed, towels laid out for showering, and the like. Between me and the black folks there was almost no conversation, not even at the hearty breakfast in the morning in a pleasant kitchen. This was Southern hospitality with caution.

SLEEPING IN PARK?

I was staying in town rather than in the park where the marchers camped overnight in a bowl-shaped area. The several hundred marchers had congregated there after the first day. In the Jesuit car which I had driven, parked back in Memphis, was the sleeping bag I had borrowed from my nephew, telling my parents I was going camping, saying nothing about the Meredith march and Deep South Mississippi, with its reputation as murderous resister of civil rights activities. They didn't have to know, I reasoned.

Without the sleeping bag, sleeping in the encampment was not a good option. In addition, we had heard tales of locals taking pot shots at us from the edge of the bowl. We also knew of cars pulling alongside and peppering white and black occupants or just clubbing them in the street, as in the 1964 "freedom summer" murders. In any case, when the call went out for those who would rather sleep in town, my hand went up. I bade adieu to my confreres and signed up for a bed in a house.

After my night in town, before resuming the day's walking, I said mass in the small local church for a few marchers, giving my homily to eight or nine people, including a Newsweek reporter from Chicago. Then it was back to the camp grounds.

I had got from Memphis to the marchers—protected by state cops since the Meredith shooting—driving with some West Side Organization dudes in a Cadillac that hit 95 m.p.h. along the way. Yes, there was Father Bowman speeding on a Mississippi highway in the company of black ex-cons. Is this what Sister Alfred and Father Regan had in mind for their eager students?

CHICAGO MARCHING

No one had to worry, it turned out. The whole business was uneventful, less dangerous than my later walks with hundreds of others in Marquette Park down Western Avenue with Martin Luther King, when he got hit by a brick. Among suspects might have been young men among whom I recognized some of my students from Ignatius who waved at me from curbside. Another of my students was part of a sort of honor guard wearing baseball mitts and catching rocks.

The Western Avenue marches had come a few days after King did an hour or so revving up us white liberals at Immanuel Lutheran Church, a few blocks from Ignatius on Ashland just north of Roosevelt. Its pastor, Don Becker, was one of the leaders of our little community organization. With King in town, in the summer of '66, churches became a focal point.

At Don Becker's church, there was excitement in the air. Before King arrived, we did a procession through the church and had our kumbaya routine. I surrendered myself so obviously to these activities that Dick Zipfel, a scholastic on the Ignatius faculty with an interest in such matters, commented on how "black" I looked, supplying irony where it was needed.

Indeed, when King arrived through a side door of the big, Gothic church, I was in the pulpit myself, warming up the folks, and did not stop immediately, which meant I could say later that I had preached while Martin Luther King listened. Jesse Jackson was with him. Jesse was making his mark in those days as a speechifying barnburner of King's calibre, if not of his calibre in any other respect. But these were the good doctor's days. He was at the center.

JUNIOR CATHOLICS

A group of high-school and early-college-age men and women were part of the congregation, which probably was no more than 100 in all. These were earnest young folk, mostly white. They included Linda, a South Sider who had been shocked to see her father defy a cop from their front porch in a racially threatened neighborhood. He and her family were resisting black encroachment—reasonably so, it turned out, because in a few years the neighborhood went all-black and crime-ridden. As of a few years ago, it had become a poster neighborhood for random killing of innocent children.

There were people to blame for that racial change, I was convinced, but today I'm not so sure. Rather, they were caught up in social change of no one's doing. Blacks and whites were fleeing black neighborhoods. No one wanted to live in them. We need only compare the Englewood crime rate today with what it was when it was white. No contest, with no one to blame but shooters and other criminals.

Linda was living with another Linda, from never racially threatened west suburban Elmhurst. Their apartment was in an old building on State Street just north of Chicago Avenue, long since replaced by a high-rise condo building. This Linda would call home, hanging up after three rings, per agreement with her mother, who would call the State Street apartment pronto, saving Linda the cost of a call, this being long before cell phones.

Hugh, my student who caught bricks in Marquette Park, was part of this group. So were several others who formed a sort of junior Catholic Interracial Council of which I was unofficial chaplain. I more or less chaperoned an overnight stay in a church, in the Cabrini Green projects neighborhood, where a Servite brother, a warm, friendly little guy who later became a Servite priest, was our host.

Breakfasting afterward in the neighborhood, I sensed hostility from the waitress about the blacks among us and got hot. That was me all over. On another occasion, at a U. of Chicago conference where the future fugitive radical Bernardine Dohrn handed out programs in a fetching mini-skirt, which I failed not to notice—she had nice gams, as movie magazines used to say—I tore into a participant who quoted Thomas Aquinas in support of his segregationist views. Such matters were being debated in those days. As too often was the case, I overdid it, shutting Sutton up and, briefly, everyone else in the crowded in-the-round meeting hall.

NEIGHBORHOOD MEETINGS

Later I provided a church-connected meeting place on the Ignatius property, in a now long gone quonset hut, for a protest meeting, not about police brutality or discrimination of any kind but about a series of burglaries in the public-housing high-rise across Roosevelt. We filled the quonset hut that night because of security concerns, which trumped the usual police-brutality and other allegations of race prejudice.

Our speaker was one of King's Southern Christian lieutenants, Rev. James Bevel, a soft-spoken, clean-cut fellow whom I ran into later at the Daily News waiting room, where he had come with some commune-like followers to quiz Bill Mauldin about a cartoon that pictured black babies as a sign of black fecklessness. On this night at Ignatius, Bevel walked into the place and gasped. "Where did they get this crowd?" he asked of no one in particular. He and King and the rest were in the business of raising consciousness, crowds, and money and knew how hard it was to draw people in the numbers such as we had drawn of our public-housing householders with their concerns about protection in their homes.

After these various meetings, most of them at churches, came the marches. "End the slums" was the slogan of the season. I wore my button in front of a Roosevelt Road polling place on election day and got called out by a bald, stocky First Ward worker. "What's that mean?" he asked, belligerent, me in my collar, both of us watched by West Side Organization worthies. I told him. He got hot and told us to get away from the polling place. We were on the south side of Roosevelt a few blocks down from Ignatius. When I didn't leave, he told the young Irish cop on duty to move me.

The First Ward man was wrong. We were neither too close to the polling place nor did we wear or carry political signs. But the cop was in a bind. He asked me to leave. We both knew that if I didn't, he'd arrest me. The ward worker had enough of a case apparently, and more important, the clout; and the young cop was not about to tell him off. He looked at me, silently pleading for me to move. That did it: I saw no cause to put him in a situation where he arrested a priest. I moved. It was a moment of truth for the WSO men, one of whom later commented that I had backed down. It was a chance for me of the white establishment to confront the (mob-connected) First Ward, and I didn't. A good thing, too.

FINGERED

My stock rose and fell with the WSO men. On my return from Mississippi or shortly after it, I was greeted on the street by one of the regulars with a handshake as "My man." But that didn't last. After our Roosevelt Road riots, a year before the Madison Street riots following King's assassination, I stood during a meeting of our little community organization, Together One Community, in a park district meeting room in the projects and bemoaned the lack of leadership in ABLA, referring obliquely to WSO and its allies.

In our midst was a weaselly fellow in a suit who told Chester Robinson, who fingered me next time he saw me on the street. His term: he was "fingering" me, which on the street meant I was in danger. A friend told me I shouldn't walk around without my collar and should watch where I walked.

I told Rev. Don Benedict about it at one of Jack Egan's meetings of the IRCUA. Benedict, a WWII conscientious objector, socialist, and pacifist, had been a co-founder in 1948 of the acclaimed East Harlem Protestant Parish, and by then was executive director of the Community Renewal Society, formerly Chicago City Missionary Society, which funded WSO with Hinsdale Union Church and other white-church money. He moved his head about in discomfort, allowing that Chester Robinson did get off base sometime, or words to that effect. There was no direct disapproval, however. Benedict and others were for self-determination and "community leadership" wherever they found it. Whether the leaders were worth supporting seemed to be moot.

GOOD TIMES

All in all, however, I liked my time in the neighborhood. I met some good people, including the storied Florence Scala, who lived on Taylor Street in back of Ignatius and had bucked Mayor Daley in his building the U. of Illinois "circle campus," smack dab where people lived. Studs Terkel gave her a chapter in the first of his immensely successful interview books, *Division Street: America*. She was a woman of deep integrity who as a girl, daughter of an immigrant tailor, had found Jane Addams' Hull House a home away from home. It was a pleasure to mix with her in these days of turmoil and excitement.

The black ministers were also a pleasure. Arthur Griffin, our little organization's treasurer who let himself be euchred by a white summer worker, later headed the historic once Congregationalist (United Church of Christ) church at Ashland and Washington, across from Union Park. The portly W.W. (Woodrow Wilson) Taylor lived well next to his substantial church near Loomis Courts, on the southwest corner of ABLA. I never begrudged him this. He was an island of middle-class achievement in the midst of trouble and was always warm and friendly.

RIOT

Indeed, it was while headed toward his church on the far side of the projects that I ran into trouble in the riots of '66, which had been set off in part by the closing of a fire hydrant on a hot day on Roosevelt Road a few blocks west of Ignatius. It was about 7 o'clock on a summer night as I made my way. I knew of the commotion that had started or was threatening. There was a meeting of concerned citizens at Taylor's church, a formidable stone structure.

I was crossing a field when a young adult Fagin who was organizing teen-agers for mischief spotted me 30 or so yards away, heading away from him and his Artful Dodgers. "Hey," he called out. I kept going, not having been born within the previous 24 hours. "Hey" again, "you with the collar." I chose not to dialogue with this group, and kept going. They did not pursue. These were kids meant for greater things, including the taunting of cops.

Later that night, after darkness fell and police and citizens were all over Roosevelt Road, a black organizer whom I knew, not of WSO, advised me to go home, my white face making too tempting a target. I did so, but not before making a white-liberal telephone call to the cops.

"This is Father Jim Bowman from St. Ignatius High School," I told the cop at the station, calling from a pay phone in the drug store at Roosevelt and Loomis. "The problem is the fire hydrants," I said. "Police turned them off on Roosevelt but not on [white] Taylor Street [a block away]. This is the problem. That's what people are mad about." (I expected him to call the squads back to the station?)

"I haven't got time for sociology," said the cop, using the catch-all (inaccurate) going term for do-goodism. So much for Father Bowman's intervention in history. I thought with supreme naivete that I was using my credentials and influence to make peace on the Near West Side. But the Fagin who yelled at me with "the collar" had other ideas. So did the men who stood behind rows of teen-agers and younger children throwing rocks at the police, as was reported to me by a young friend.

Next day, another friend showed up on the street with an arm in a sling. We talked at Roosevelt and Loomis. He wouldn't be going to work that day in a far suburb, partly because of the broken or bruised arm, what a cop had apparently done to him in a melee, partly because he was afraid to show himself, a black guy, in a white enclave after the previous night's rioting.

END GAME

This gives a flavor of life at Ignatius after teaching. It was going to end. I knew that. My free-lancing from retreat to retreat was no life for me. I was fairly directionless, without assignment. I talked about it with Harvanek, who suggested Xavier University, Cincinnati, where I would be an English teacher. Fact is, if I hadn't been saddled with my itch to change the world and my specific itch to achieve racial justice, I'd have wanted nothing better. He probably did more than suggest. It didn't matter. I was ready to do something else, even if it meant leaving Chicago behind. And teaching English on a college campus? Just what the vocation doctor ordered.

I told people on the street I was leaving, including Chester Robinson, who chided me, implying that I'd been appreciated and it was a shame I would no longer be on the scene. He regretted my leaving, he said, the two of us having dismissed or even forgotten his fingering me months earlier. Maybe Don Benedict had said something.

DECLINING FINAL APPROVAL

Meanwhile, in addition to my street-roaming, I had taken over the summer enrichment program started by Jack Arnold and other scholastics and had run it for two summers, using federal "anti-poverty" money that I applied for and was given gladly, because the givers were confident we wouldn't waste it. My work on the program included driving a big school bus, taking boys to places where they would not go otherwise. But it was mainly my oversight of classroom work, recruiting teachers and students with a view to improving their reading and writing. I was in the midst of that, in the summer of '66, when I heard from the provincial about my final vows, corrected the "clerical error" that had told me during tertianship that I wouldn't have that to decide for another 18 months, and scheduled it for the Ignatius Jesuit community chapel.

Brother Bob Cardosi planned a festive breakfast afterward for me and my parents and whoever else came for the occasion, which would have a somewhat muted but still palpable solemnity. For my pre-vows retreat, I went out to North Aurora, where my alma mater, West Baden College, had been relocated in a converted Holiday Inn and was known by then as Bellarmine College. It was my annual eight-day retreat, which as a priest I would make on my own, pursuing the Spiritual Exercises with my accumulated 16 years of wisdom and presumed expertise.

I had the final vows to consider, of course. I probed them at length, subjecting them to more scrutiny than they could survive, at least for my purposes. The provincial, John Connery, came by Bellarmine while I was there. He and I sat on a bench to talk. I asked him what these final vows added to the vows I'd already taken. He spoke of increased solemnity, as I recall, somehow more solemn than the ones I already had.

Connery, a moral theologian of international repute, was not about to b.s. me. In my opinion, he said what there was to say. It came down to the ceremonial aspect of life in religion, for one thing, something I do not lightly dismiss. Our lives are full of ceremony and would be lessened without them. We may call it the devotional aspect, and neither do I dismiss acts of devotion. Indeed, I have come to rely on them in my Sunday mass attendance, which has generally served to remind me of my belief and strengthen it.

These final vows, simple or solemn, also tied me and the society together more tightly, psychologically (as above, through ceremony) but also legally, in that they made it more difficult in canon law for us to split from each other. That probationary aspect again. Final vows were the society's seal of approval and my act of renewed commitment. This had nothing to do with my being a priest, which had its own Vatican-connected rules. Vows had to do with me and the Jesuits, the general's office in Rome being where authority lay. The pope had charge of me as a priest, the general, or "black pope," of me as a Jesuit.

So the society was ready to give me final approval, but I was on the ropes or at least staggering. I was dizzy with weakened commitment to religious life and strengthened feelings toward being married. I was in process of alienation from my life as a priest and Jesuit. Months later, when I told a long-time friend I was leaving, he asked me what I was to do for my identity? I said I had long before lost my sense of Jesuit identity. (I was wrong: To a degree, I had let it grow dormant.)

This was too bad. During the coming year at Ignatius, I was to be asked by a fellow activist as he was dropped me off at Ignatius after a meeting, how I managed as a celibate. I stayed busy, I told him. I stayed distracted, I might have said.

He was a very genial guy, ethnically Jewish, who wished me "Merry Christmas" with a great smile. Later he sent my wife and me Christmas pictures of him and his wife and kids—his wife was not Jewish—looking contented and middle-class, no matter his saying once that he and others were in the process of turning my white collar "red." He was the first person I ever heard dismiss democracy as a vehicle of justice. (The second was a fellow newspaper reporter.) Later he gave me as a reference for a government job. By then he was on his way to becoming a Unitarian and member of the local

Democratic organization in a Western city—both being homes for aging leftists, in my experience.

ON TO CINCINNATI

Meanwhile, the summer program completed and my paper work in the hands of the Office of Economic Opportunity downtown, I packed my trunk and bags one August day and decamped for Cincinnati to teach English. I was a late appointment; but Tom Savage, who headed the Xavier University English department, found three slots for me. I had to bone up on my poetry for an evening class of business majors and others, whom I intended to make a little more sensitive to the finer things in life.

In the class was Bill Mason, a black guy known around Xavier and in the neighborhood as stand-up and congenial, a 20-something bachelor and guardian of a teen-age nephew. He and I played basketball and ate pizza and drank beer together. He took me into black bars and in general helped make life more familiar and comfortable in my new home.

On campus I lived in the so-called honors dormitory, a three-story mansion, a gift to the university and thus in no way scarred by dormitory architecture or design. It housed mostly honors course students. As a high school senior many years earlier, I had been considered for and had considered entering the Xavier honors program. I fielded at least one telephone call at the time from Father Heatherington, who ran the program then and was running it 18 years later when I went to live in the dorm. I did not go to Xavier but to Loyola. My generation of our family was the first to attend college, and leaving town for school was not accepted procedure.

As dorm rector, I was in the midst of students, living in my own first-floor room with fridge and pantry. I shared the latter two with an older Jesuit, a very nice guy who taught theology. Between us we had our own car. Moreover, at XU you only had to go to the common supply room in the main Jesuit residence, a fort-like structure on a hill in the center of campus, to replenish your liquor supply. Not bad. Between my bedroom and the rather extensive hallway entrance area was an anteroom where I had a desk and telephone and typewriter.

DEATH AND BURIAL

On November 1, 1967, I was sitting in that anteroom office with a female student, going over her work, the outer door wisely kept open, when the phone rang. It was my brother in Chicago saying our father had died. He had dropped by his and my mother's Oak Park apartment in the middle of a work day, between calls on customers for a printing company, had gone into the bathroom and hadn't come out. My mother pushed the door but couldn't get it all the way open because he had slipped off the toilet and was leaning against it. An occlusion had done it, as it had done to his younger sister Enid some years earlier at 63. He was 72. The brother who called with the news went the same way, 30 years later, at 73. Circulation was quick death for some in our family, in the blink of an eye.

I drove to Chicago for the wake and funeral. The wake went two nights, was packed each night—a tremendous outpouring for my father, whose memory meant much to those he left behind. My mother revived nicely for it, buoyed as ever by the socializing, to which she always responded with her sparkling smile and conversation.

Back at XU after wake and funeral, I continued my brand of outreach to the neighborhood. I had gone looking for activity but did not find anything right away. I did make contact eventually with some white activists who gathered and devised a plan of deployment in case of rioting, which was in the air. And I found and went to meetings, standing at one of them at a microphone somewhat foolishly waving my membership card in the Association of Chicago Priests. Someone asked me later if my XU superiors had sat on me for that appearance. It had never occurred to me that they would, and they didn't.

While attending another meeting later in the spring, word came of King's being shot, and we went into action in our assigned roles and places.

CHAPTER 8. CHECKING OUT: CINCINNATI & DENOUEMENT, 1967–68

For when the One Great Scorer comes
To mark against your name,
He writes not that you won or lost,
But how you played the game.
—Grantland Rice

The end was approaching. I had arrived at XU with a fresh start, teaching English, my first enthusiasm as a teacher. Tom Savage as head of the department found classes for me and halfway through the semester asked if I was up to teaching honors English in the coming summer and thenceforward in the fall. It was fine with me. Things couldn't be working out better.

At the honors students dorm of which I became rector, I greeted one non-honors student (a few were inserted in the midst), a few years older than the others, arriving several sheets to the wind one night and next day informed him he could move pronto to another dorm. I may have said the same to one or two others, but in any case I spotted morale holes and plugged them, presto-change-o, helping to make the honors dorm a very good place to be.

But I was allowing my frustration at living a bachelor existence to determine my general attitude. I also had my social, especially racial, justice itch to contend with, which was not all bad, of course. I got close to some black football players, and when it came time for the compulsory students' retreat, I volunteered to give it to the black athletes. We met in the chapel or some other meeting room, and I organized a few days of supposed retreat for them.

Later I sat with them and a visiting black academic from California who looked like a footballer himself but had revolution on his mind. At one point in the conversation, with a half dozen XU blacks and me in the room, the visitor looked to the students and asked if I was "all right." They, surprised as I at the question and not especially of revolutionary bent, said yes, and he spoke in vague terms of armed rebellion. I just sat there.

It was the sort of thing you heard those days. Sally, a Lutheran-church-connected community worker out of a Milwaukee suburb, was asked by a "community leader" if she would help blacks get guns. It wasn't what she had in mind, neither was it what I had in mind. Sally made that clear. I never quite had to, but I was skating close to the edge of really dumb involvement.

JESUITS I LIVED WITH

Within the Jesuit community, I found a sympathetic guy in the minister—the man in charge of supplies and all physical requirements, from cars to liquor cabinet. This was Gene Helmick, whom I had known at Ignatius when he was pastor of Holy Family Church. He cherished no illusions about anything and had frank, wry comments about the Holy Family neighborhood, once characterizing a Taylor Street (Italian) storefront "social and athletic club" as a place where for the boys and girls it was "zip, zip, and into each other."

Neither did he have illusions about the XU community, with whose drinking and other habits he was familiar. Later, while still a Jesuit, he got a counseling certificate from Menninger Clinic in Kansas for which he wrote a clinical-psychological description of the community that the Menninger people refused to believe. Do it over, they told him. He did, and they still couldn't believe it but took his word for it. Their solution was to break that community up and start over, he told me.

I did have my minor run-ins with the university president, Paul O'Connor, who like Mike English had been a high-ranking military chaplain (I think Navy) in World War II. He had been aboard the battleship Missouri for the signing of surrender by the Japanese, I heard. Paul was a rangy, athletic guy, good-looking and possessing a fine presence for his position.

The university was a major fixture in Cincinnati life, more than Loyola was in Chicago. The city also had U. of Cincinnati, of course, which dwarfed XU but seemed to have less influence. Cincinnati is heavily Catholic, for one thing, and the Jesuits had been there a long time. There was also the downtown Jesuit parish, St. Xavier's, and its high school, St. Xavier High (X-High), which had moved to the city's outskirts in spacious new building and grounds a few years earlier.

SENT TO THE KITCHEN

That said, and whether from Navy experience or the Germanic Cincinnati sense of orderliness—even the Irish were Germanized in Cincinnati, said my brother Jerry—Paul ran a ship that was tight in ways I was not used to from my days at Ignatius. For instance, I walked over to the main residence for my first meal on arrival wearing a sport shirt, which was standard at Ignatius in the summer time. But a Jesuit some 10 years older than I, a Chicagoan who had some responsibility in the matter, spotted me and steered me into the kitchen to eat. Why? Because at XU you wore cassock to meals. There was to be no sitting down and realizing I was out of place or even (with a smile?) reminding me of how it was done there: it was to the scullery with me, where I sat with cooks and helpers eyeing me with barely concealed grins. Wasn't that a nice welcome!

Litanies were big also. These were the 15 minutes or so of group prayer in the chapel before dinner, an exercise in rote petition which I knew from novitiate days. I skipped litanies and decided not to hide it, planting myself at the rector's table as "the monks" filed in for grace before meal. O'Connor made a crack on this occasion, as he did later about the length of my hair, in this case as indirect critique of my non-observance.

Smarting from this but not smart enough to ignore it, I went to see him the next day and said I found litanies harmful to my prayer life (such as it was, I should have said) and would not be attending. A day or so later, I retracted that, deciding there was no point in making an issue of it. He seemed impervious both times, and indeed when all was said and done, was someone for whose demeanor I could have nothing but respect. Like Mike English, he was an earlier generation of Jesuit who were direct and, I should say, manly. There was nothing nervous about him.

PROTESTING THE POLICE

On another, more substantive occasion, I signed my name to a protest statement that got play in the Cincinnati Enquirer. It was a fairly mild protest, by me and maybe ten other church-related locals, of how police handled antiwar protestors who had come down from Antioch (Ohio) College in early December. That was our complaint, how the police handled the situation, dragging a protestor down courthouse stairs by his hair, and the like. It was not about the war as such, about which I remained ambivalent, though generally suspicious.

As I said before, I hadn't studied it, as I had studied the race question, nor had I been there, as I had been on the race scene. Neither had I been at the scene of the Cincinnati protest but read and heard eyewitness accounts that convinced me: the cops had used a hammer for the fly on baby's nose, it seemed to me. We church liberals got together, worked out a statement, and sent it off.

I saw it in the paper and called Paul O'Connor right away, before he had seen it, because I didn't want him blindsided any more than he was by my not consulting him in the first place. I had not even considered consulting him, but as one of his people who had gone public in a sensitive matter, I thought he deserved to know, before benefactors and the like came at him. He was as good about it as I could have asked. "Do you know what you're doing?" he asked me. "Yes, Paul," I said. "I've been informed in detail about it and do know." OK, he said. No fulmination, no sign of upset. He seemed less exercised by this than about my abstaining from litanies.

Meanwhile, toward the end of the semester, I had more to think about than Paul O'Connor or Antioch students. My vocation problems were taking over my thinking. I discussed them with a contemporary with counseling credentials who lived in a high-rise dorm while plying his counseling trade. I described my situation to him. Beset by the demon sexual desire, I was looking ahead to a rocky road of survival and risk. It was risky business, this being unmarried. I was distracted and unable to come to terms with the life I had chosen, indeed had reached the point where the only thing keeping me back was how my mother would react. Not a good enough reason, he said. And that probably tipped it.

DEPARTURE PLANNING

It was better to marry than to burn, as St. Paul said. I decided I was not for burning. I told the provincial, Bob Harvanek, the same whose philosophy classes were one of the bright spots along the way. He suggested outside counseling, which I thought was a good idea. I went to a man in Cincinnati who asked a lot of questions, including whether I wanted to discuss my situation with a priest.

Negative to that one, because I felt I couldn't trust a priest not to tilt toward my staying—though I had just gotten open-minded advice from a priest-professional. I decided to stay with this fellow, which I did, all expenses paid. The Jesuits did things right, even when one of theirs was jumping ship.

Meanwhile, I called Tom Savage and resigned from the English Department. With weeks to go before start of the second semester. "Well, Jim, that's a hell of a note," he said, reasonably. "I know it is, Tom, and I'll tell you about it some day." That took care of that. John Felten, a Jesuit some 20 years my senior, and long on the XU faculty, hearing that I was loose, came at me with a great idea: I should become XU's man for the neighborhood. He was impressed with the need to relate to the outside. I would be liaison. I ridiculously put it to Paul O'Connor, who again was reasonable: "Jim, you resign from the faculty, leaving those duties hanging, and now you want me to appoint you to represent us in a sensitive area?" I told him he was right. End of that idea.

Harvanek suggested I go crosstown to St. Xavier High, where there was a part-time hole in the faculty I could fill. Good. I had friends there of my age and tenure in the society, not to mention scholastics, with whom I had more in common than with most of the XU Jesuits. I moved out of the honors dorm and went to the high school.

The university newspaper interviewed me. Was my leaving Xavier related to my signing the protest or my other activities? Not at all, I said, speaking the truth. It was easy to shoot that one down, and I heard later that the XU Jesuits appreciated that from me. Not all Jesuits were going as quietly into the night. One in Detroit got splashed all over the papers, having gone to Rome to protest his treatment by superiors. I knew him for a tremendous athlete, smart as hell, an impulsive, outgoing personality. The air was full of this sort of thing.

Another, who had been our "spiritual father" as a second-year novice when we entered in 1950, left quietly but wrote a letter to everyone he knew explaining why. I tucked that in the back of mind and later did likewise.

ASSASSINATION AND RIOT

I slipped away from XU to the high school on the edge of town, where I found a younger, more congenial community by far, headed as rector by none other than Tom Murray, the genial, easy-going but strong principal at Loyola Academy whom I had found a relief after my first year under Rudy Knoepfle. Two Jesuits I had been ordained with, and with whom I had ridden the train down to Cincinnati in August 1950, were on the faculty. One of the scholastics had been a student and sodality member when I'd taught at Loyola Academy. There were others I knew. It was old home week. I settled in with an abbreviated teaching schedule and other activities, including my weekly sessions with the shrink.

I stayed in contact with my activist friends in the city, remaining in the loop with regard to deployment of our rapid-response team in case of riots. The cities were erupting. We figured our role was to be on hand helping achieve peace with justice as the saying goes. We were not running guns, as the black guy proposed to the church worker Sally. But we would be on hand in other capacities. The occasion arose when King was shot, and Cincinnati had its riot, a mini-riot compared to Chicago, where Madison Street became a river of fire.

I heard about the assassination at a meeting. My assignment was night court, where rioters would be brought. I sat in my clerics in the front row taking notes and glaring at the judge when I thought it necessary. (Later he complained to Paul O'Connor about me.)

The dozen or so arrested citizens were all black but one. They seemed a feckless group rather than dangerous. The judge was stern and unbending. I wrote what I saw. It became a sort of *samizdat*, copied and passed around and even used as supplementary reading material for a history class at a Catholic women's college in town.

Eventually it ran as a cover story in Ave Maria magazine, a national weekly. I had submitted it to that publication on my arrival as an associate editor straight out of the Jesuits. Indeed, I edited it for publication. My account, as dispassionate and baldly descriptive as I could make it, was of that night court on the night of the riots—a "drumhead court," I called it.

Once it had gone to the press room downstairs, a printer came up and came to me at my desk. "This stuff you write about," he asked, grimy from setting type. "You saw it happen?" When I said yes, he walked away shaking his head, not as objection to me but to the procedures in the courtroom.

A Cincinnati Enquirer columnist castigated me for it. The church worker Sally wrote to say my "S.J.," stood for "swinger for justice."

FINDING A JOB

But before that happened, I had my own row to hoe. Looking towards my departure, I put feelers out for public-school teaching jobs and gave Tom Savage as a reference. Sav, who was in the dark about my plans, asked Tom Murray, the rector, what was up. Murray, also in the dark, asked me. I told him I was leaving. "Have you got a bishop?" he asked, that is, was I remaining a priest but joining a diocese? No, I was leaving completely. "Have you got a job?" he asked.

How do you like that? I'm walking out of everything and his first concern is whether I was employed. No, I said, mentioning some aspects of my search and adding that there was a Catholic Press Association convention in Columbus, a few hours' drive away, where something might be available. "You ought to go there," he said, and so I went, driving up and introducing myself as Father Jim Bowman looking for a job.

"See John Reedy," people told me. This was the Holy Cross priest who was editor of Ave Maria, a national Catholic weekly based at University of Notre Dame. Reedy and I talked, and a week or two later sealed our deal by telephone. I would be associate editor at $8,000 a year.

DEPARTURE

Finally, my day came to depart. The night before, I sat in the kitchen having a beer with some of the community, including Jim Brichetto, a solidly built, husky guy, a Cincinnatian teaching at his alma mater, from which he had gone directly to Milford years earlier. He had seen his life's opportunity and taken it. Rough-hewn and a scholar by default, he ruled the classroom like a colossus, pounding Latin into the heads of his students.

As a scholastic at Ignatius, he had the swim team, whom he would drive in a bus for practice at a nearby YMCA. One of the boys yelled at some black kids on the way back one day, and Brichetto stopped the bus and made him get off. Apparently nothing happened to the kid, at least worth telling anyone.

On my last night, Brichetto and I and two or three others had a good hour or so chatting in the kitchen over a beer. As we broke up, he commented that this is how we Jesuits should get together with each other, referring to our relaxed camaraderie. Next morning after breakfast, five or six gathered at the loading dock to say goodbye to me.

My rental car was waiting, compliments of the Xavier U. minister, who also gave me $400 for the pocket. I was good to go, as people say. As we stood there, joshing briefly, Brichetto, who was not one I'd told of my leaving, passed the area and looked out at me from some 75 feet away, me in civvies and obviously on my way. We caught each other's eye.

He had a slightly bewildered look I had never seen on him—like Jesus being led away by Roman soldiers, looking at Peter, who had denied him. Way in the back of my head, it was occurring to me that I was betraying him. I wondered momentarily, how many others?

The feeling disappeared and did not return. I was off to my new life, simultaneously apprehensive and exhilarated.

ABOUT THE AUTHOR:

Jim Bowman covered religion for the Chicago Daily News from 1968 to its closing in 1978, has written or edited thirteen books, working out of his home in Oak Park, Illinois, where he and his wife raised their six children.

His 1994 book, *Bending the Rules: What American Priests Tell American Catholics* (Crossroad), has interviews with dozens of veteran pastors coast to coast.

Other books include corporate histories of Booz Allen and Hamilton and Rush-Presbyterian-St. Luke's Medical Center.

For three years in the early '80s he did a weekly column, "The Way We Were," for the Chicago Tribune.

More recently he edited C. Paul Johnson's book, *Good Guys Finish First: Reflections of a CEO and How to Start a Community Bank* (Xlibris, 2004).

He is a columnist for the online publication, Chicago Catholic News, and blogs at Blithe Spirit, Chicago Newspapers, and other sites.